Brave Girl Boots

A Forty-Day
Journey to Brave

TAMI WALKER

WESTBOW°
PRESS
A DIVISION OF THOMAS NELSON
& ZONDERVAN

Scripture quotations taken from The Amplified Bible, Copyright ©1954,1958,1962,1964,1965,1987 by The Lockman Foundation. Used by permission.

Scripture quotations marked "ESV" are taken from The Holy Bible, English Standard Version. Copyright © 2000; 2001 by Crossway Bibles, a division of Good News Publishers. Used by permission. All rights reserved.

GOD'S WORD is a copyrighted work of God's Word to the Nations. Quotations are used by permission. Copyright © 1995 by God's Word to the Nations. All rights reserved.

Scripture quotations from THE MESSAGE. Copyright © by Eugene H. Peterson 1993, 1994, 1995, 1996, 2000, 2001, 2002. Used by permission of NavPress Publishing Group.

Scripture taken from the New American Standard Bible, © Copyright 1960, 1962,1963, 1968,1971,1973,1975,1977 by The Lockman Foundation. Used by permission.

All Scripture quotations, unless otherwise indicated, are taken from the Holy Bible, New International Version®, Copyright © 1973, 1978, 1984 by International Bible Society. Used by permission of Zondervan. All rights reserved.

Scripture taken from the New King James Version. Copyright © 1982 by Thomas Nelson, Inc. Used by permission. All rights reserved.

Scripture quotations marked (NLT) are taken from the Holy Bible, New Living Translation, copyright © 1996. Used by permission of Tyndale House Publishers, Inc., Wheaton, IL 60189 USA. All rights reserved.

WestBow Press books may be ordered through booksellers or by contacting:

WestBow Press
A Division of Thomas Nelson & Zondervan
1663 Liberty Drive
Bloomington, IN 47403
www.westbowpress.com
1 (866) 928-1240

Because of the dynamic nature of the Internet, any web addresses or links contained in this book may have changed since publication and may no longer be valid. The views expressed in this work are solely those of the author and do not necessarily reflect the views of the publisher, and the publisher hereby disclaims any responsibility for them.

ISBN: 978-1-4908-7809-6 (sc)
ISBN: 978-1-4908-7811-9 (hc)
ISBN: 978-1-4908-7810-2 (e)

Library of Congress Control Number: 2015906627

Print information available on the last page.

WestBow Press rev. date: 05/28/2015

This book is dedicated to my niece, Kaitlyn. I'm very proud of you. You've put your brave girl boots on and determined to not let your past tell your future what it should do.

Foreword

Tami Walker is the consummate definition of a "brave boots girl." When Christ got hold of her, He really got hold of her! She left a successful career in the marketplace and entered vocational ministry because she believed that God had a call on her life.

It's been my joy to work side-by-side with Tami for the last nine years, not just as the pastor of Connection Church, but also as her friend. During that time, I have watched her blossom and develop spiritually and relationally while developing a mature and consistent faith. Her passion for ministry and connecting people to God, friends, and service is constant, tangible, and heartfelt.

Being a rigorous reader herself, Tami has now crafted something that will touch the hearts of many women. *Brave Girl Boots: A Forty-Day Journey to Brave* is a wonderful chronicle of the real-life stories of some of Tami's brave girlfriends.

You will be touched both spiritually and emotionally as you read the stories that helped shape these ladies' lives. Each story is unique, but all reflect God's love, grace, and faithfulness.

In combining life experiences with Scripture, Tami has painted a canvas that begs to be examined. The challenge will be for her readers to read just one story per day. That's the game plan of a forty-day devotional. But honestly, I can't help but think of the old LAY'S potato chip commercial that taunted its viewers with the tagline, "Betcha can't eat just one."

For those of you who are able to parcel the devotional over its intended time, each of these forty mini symphonies of God's grace cascades into a resounding orchestra of praise to our Heavenly Father. Knowing Tami, I'm pretty certain that was her construct from the beginning.

So sit back, and grab a good book—oops, you already did—and enjoy your trek as you see God revealed in the details of the lives of some very special ladies.

In Christ,
Rocky Barra
Lead Pastor
Connection Church

Acknowledgments

To Cal Walker, my husband, my leader, my comic relief—not only did you champion this project, but you also saw the gifts God has given me and spoke them into life. You show me Jesus every single day. I'm so proud to be your wife.

To the brave women in this book who shared their stories of brave and not-so-brave moments—thank you, thank you, thank you! You inspire me daily.

To the CGgirls (Common Ground Girls) Leadership Team: Kelly Bates, Liz Clark and Nora Syracuse—I can't think of a greater team with which to take God's love from the pews to the pavement. Thank you for your faithful commitment to kingdom building and your friendship.

To the people at Connection Church—you are a safe harbor for anyone looking for shelter from the storms of life. I can't imagine running my race of faith with anyone else. Thank you for believing in this project and me. A special thank you to the man who put money in my hand one Sunday and said, "This is for your book project; I believe in you." You know who you are.

To Debi Hawn for bathing this project in prayer—you are the unsung hero of this book. Thank you for all the times you reminded me that God was leading this and not me.

To Brittany Ball of B Leigh Photography for blessing us with your talents and capturing our perfect book cover—thank you for your generous spirit and commitment to excellence.

To Gen Lizyness—you loved me to Jesus. Thank you for taking the time to not only tell me about the Lord, but also show me how He loves. Who knows where I would be without those late conversations at AAA.

I am grateful for my parents, Gene and Dodi Frailey. You gave me a safe place to grow and thrive. I love you both!

To my beloved pastor and his wife, Rocky and Nancy Barra—you will never know, this side of heaven, the impact you've made on my life and thousands of others. You bleed grace.

Finally, I am forever grateful for Jesus Christ, my faithful and true King. You gave me life when I deserved death. Forever You reign in my heart and life. You make me brave.

Little Brave Heart

One woman fears
The creep of old age;
Another one fears
The remnants of rage.

This one fears
The ravages of cancer,
And that one there fears
The pregnancy test answer.

She lives in worry
That love will not find her
While she dreads the future
And the promise that bound her.

She worries at night
As her womb grows and swells,
But her crib sits there, empty,
And her pain is not quelled.

She helplessly watches
As her prospects diminish
While she fears the Devil
With her is not finished.

This mother fears
For her child's unknown fate,
And this one is weary
Of her ex-husband's hate.

But there is One who feels every cut, every slice.
His flesh hung in ribbons while soldiers played dice.
No fear you have equals the whip lined with lead;
No loss you feel now like the sin on His head.
Betrayal, rejection, and hurt feelings dismissed
Are specks in a storm next to Judas' last kiss.
No road has been traveled His feet have not tread,
No painful condition His mercy can't thread.
All your fears and your sorrows He remembers and knows.
Drop your fear in love's river that rushes and flows.
He took your fears with Him when He triumphed the grave.
Rise up, all you sisters! And choose to be brave!

Written by Cal Walker

Brave girl—yes, you. No need to look over your shoulder—I'm talking to you, brave girl. When I call you brave, how does that make you feel inside? Do you smile and sit up a bit taller? Or did you immediately smirk, thinking, *Me? Brave? That's unlikely.* Be honest. It's just you and me. We may not know each other, but I believe we have more in common than you think. Don't believe me? Trust me when I say I understand unlikely.

When I look up the word *unlikely* in the dictionary, I find this definition: "not likely to happen, be done, or be true; improbable." My whole life has been one big unlikely. You think I'm kidding?

I was raised in a good home, but Jesus and attending church were not part of my upbringing. It wasn't until I was thirty-one years old that I put my faith in Jesus Christ. Researchers would say that's pretty unlikely.

After walking with the Lord for five years, I left my career of eighteen years and went into full-time ministry. I would have told you that's extremely unlikely.

I was a forty-five-year-old, never-married, single woman. The chances of me getting married were pretty unlikely. On August 3, 2013, that all changed.

One of my life's greatest privileges has been leading a movement of women called CGgirls. The heartbeat of CGgirls is to encourage women to be kingdom builders by taking God's love from the pews to the pavement. We gather four times a year at an event called Common Ground, a cross-denominational event for women. When CGgirls started in 2009, I was told by several people, "It's unlikely women from other churches will be involved with this; it just won't happen. People aren't really as kingdom minded as they say they are." In January 2014, we hosted our twentieth event with over two hundred women from thirty-four different churches in attendance. How is that for unlikely?

The common thread through my entire life has been unlikely. But do you know who shows up to bring likely smack-dab in the middle of my unlikely? Jesus Christ. I love that Jesus chooses to use the unlikely for His glory. Remember the twelve men Jesus hung out with? Yeah, pretty unlikely. First Corinthians 1:27 shares this truth: "But God chose the foolish things of the world to shame the wise; God chose the weak things of the world to shame the strong."

What I'm also learning to be true is that God is above human opinion. It doesn't matter what diagnosis you may receive, what words have wounded you, or how sure you are that you don't measure up—God has the final say in everything.

Brave girl, are we on the same page yet with our unlikeliness? We can keep our focus on our unlikely, but it won't take us anywhere. We'll stay stuck and fearful. There *is* a better way.

His name is Jesus. Jesus Christ is trustworthy, steadfast, and true. He knows our very nature is to be fearful; nothing is hidden from Him. He knows He is the answer—and honestly, most days, *we* know He is the answer. But on any given day, despite what we know, there is a good chance we'll operate out of fear, certainly not out of a place of faith.

Brave girl, regardless of what the enemy of our lives would tell us, fear is not in fashion. Yet we keep trying it on. Think of fear as a pair of skinny jeans. They look different on everyone.

One of the ways I believe I have operated out of fear has been my endless pursuit to remove all unknowns from my life. Isn't that foolishness? It is tiring as well. How much control do I really think I have over the big picture of my life? Apparently, not enough! My husband, Cal, discovered my need-to-know quirkiness early on in our dating relationship. He would eagerly agree with me on this. Only minutes into watching a movie, the questions would come. "What's going to happen?" "How does this end?" "Who dies?"

Finally, one day, my very patient man looked at me and said, "Why can't you just let it unfold and enjoy the journey?" Ouch! As soon as those words left Cal's mouth, they hit my heart. I felt a little nudge from God. *Okay, okay, okay! Teach me how to enjoy the journey, Lord!*

To be honest, brave girl, God has pretty much let me know that my future is none of my business. Apparently, my life is on a need-to-know basis with Him. You too? When I need to know; He'll fill me in, *and it drives me crazy!* But I'm learning, and God is patient—very patient.

What about you? What does fear look like on you?

Do you wrestle with the fear of people? When my relationship with Jesus started and I was still trying to figure this whole thing out, I was always fearful I would walk by faith and then be stuck hanging there. Would God forget about me? Would I look like an idiot to others—or at least to my friends? What about my reputation?

Brave girl, I have wonderful news. In fact, it's better than wonderful; it's fantastic. In Psalm 86:15, we find this awesome piece of good news: "But you, Lord, are a compassionate and gracious God, slow to anger, abounding in love and faithfulness." Did you catch this? He abounds. Last time I checked, *abounds* meant "a lot." That's a whole lot of love and faithfulness.

It is possible to trade our fears for the faithfulness of God. If we are a child of God, there is no reason to fear the unknown or people. We can stand on the faithfulness of God. (If you are unsure whether you are a child of God, you can turn to the back of the book to find out more.)

How about it, brave girl? Let's take the next forty days and travel together on this highway of faith with the Lord! Who doesn't love a good road trip?

If you are thinking, *Forty days? How is God going to change my fear to faith in just forty days?* I want to challenge your thinking. What if you began to view bravery through God's eyes? I once thought I had to be brave for God, but now I know He wants me to be brave with Him.

Jesus, so full of compassion toward us that we will never fully understand this side of heaven, extends His hands to us. We aren't asked to do this solo. Yes, we live our lives for Jesus, but the real treasure is that we get to do this with Jesus. Look at what Micah 6:8 (NASB) says. "He has told you, O man, what is good; and what does the Lord require of you but to do justice, to love kindness, and to walk humbly with your God?" Did you catch that? With God. You aren't in this alone, brave girl.

Being brave looks a lot more doable when we remember that God is with us. Do you agree?

Maybe you are still trying to figure out who Jesus is or have walked with the Lord for years. I believe wholeheartedly that you are not reading this book by accident. Let's get those brave girl boots out, dust them off, and take God at His Word.

Do you want to hear something completely comforting? Jesus knows your fear. Would you be willing over the next forty days to take the hand of grace He extends to you and begin a journey of discovery?

Christ promises to never leave or forsake us. I think a promise from the Most High God holds a bit more weight than a pinkie swear.

If you are struggling to put on your brave girl boots, I promise you that you are not alone. Living the life Jesus has planned for you is worth the struggle. The beautiful moment in time we call *today* should not be wasted. For reasons I still can't fully comprehend, God wants to use our lives to bring Him glory. He wants to use us—messy, wounded people.

Over the next forty days, we'll start each day together. Who's bringing the coffee? Just kidding—kind of.

I've invited some other brave girls to join us, too. I hope you don't mind. They will be sharing their own personal stories of bravery and not-so-brave moments. It'll be you, me, other brave girls, and of course, Jesus. Remember, we aren't doing this without Him.

Brave girl, I'm just like you. Trust me. I'm learning to be brave. It's a slow process, but one God is wooing me to. I read today on Facebook, "Comfort zones are peaceful, but you won't grow there." I want to grow. How about you?

While you're finding your brave girl boots (try under the bed or behind the couch), I want to share a story about something God did through CGgirls.

I remember it like it was yesterday. When I first heard about these unwanted, troubled girls in foster care, my heart was stirred. What must being unwanted feel like? My mind caught up with my stirred heart and began dreaming with God.

How can we show these girls far from God they are valued, adored, and known? My mind got to thinking, and my heart got to praying. The answer came quickly; CGgirls would adopt these fourteen girls for Christmas and blow their minds. We sincerely felt that because God loves all of us with extravagant grace, we wanted to back up our "Jesus loves you" with a Christmas they would never forget. Project Crazy Love (PCL) was born.

We knew an event of this scale would not only need a whole bunch of hearts, but also a whole bunch of hands. The planning and dreaming began. At our summer Common Ground event, we put a shocking pink Christmas tree up in our after party area. Can you picture it? Our Project Crazy Love tree was filled with gift tags for each girl. More than 1,200 gift tags hung on that tree. Women began to take not one, but several gift tags. Brave girl, sometimes you have to go with what you know and trust God to fill in the gaps—and did He ever! CGgirls donated 1,240 gifts for those fourteen girls.

There is no question in my mind that the generous spirit unleashed through CGgirls was authored by God! Women were chasing me down with such fantastic generosity that it often left me speechless and always in tears. Watching God work in such big ways on behalf of girls far from Him always leaves me humbled and hungry. I'm humbled by His love and hungry for more of Him.

CGgirls worked hard shopping, wrapping, and preparing for our PCL Christmas lunch. We didn't have much to go on other than a name and age for each girl. On the big day, as the sun was rising, it became clear the Son was all over this event. With all the other Christmas gifts hidden out of sight, the elf team put one gift for each girl under the pink Christmas tree.

In the center of the room, we put the bodacious pink Christmas tree, and instead of the gift tags that hung a few months prior, we hung notecards. On the outside, each had the name of a PCL girl; inside was a note of encouragement and love.

Honestly, I thought that would be the last thing to grab their attention. They are teenage girls, and I figured the gifts would be the main event. I was wrong. As it turned, out the notes were the highlight of the event. Even as I recall it today, my eyes sting with tears.

The girls arrived, and I was immediately taken aback by how young and innocent they looked. I'm not sure what I was expecting, but this wasn't it. Their ages ranged from twelve to eighteen. They looked like little girls.

When our guests of honor came into the Christmas lunch room and saw fourteen gifts under the tree, they squealed with delight. I'm sure we all thought the same thing: *Just you wait!* We all enjoyed a wonderful lunch and desserts (complete with a chocolate fountain and cotton candy). Once our tummies were full, I mentioned to the PCL girls that they could get their notecards from the tree. Excited to get the cards, they raced over to the tree. My heart was silenced with what I witnessed next. Remember how I thought the cards would be the least impactful? I couldn't have been more wrong.

What took place next was the absolute highlight of the day for me. Each of these young women, far from God, was about to see how close God really was to her. As the girls opened up their notecards, we heard them say, "I've never gotten a card in my life." "How could someone know what I was going through?" "They wrote this like they knew me. How can they know me?" The majority of them sobbed (ugly crying here, brave girls!) as they read the precious life-giving words CGgirls wrote to them.

I sat there in fantastic awe of our God. He shined the spotlight on our basic need to be known. It was a humbling moment. In a world that had cast these beautiful young girls aside and labeled them unwanted with no value, God broke through those labels. He reminded them there is a God who sees, knows, loves, and waits.

It was an honor to witness this sacred moment. It was so intimate that at times, I found myself looking away. They were being ministered to by Jesus, and it made me blush. God poured healing balm into their hearts, and it left the room quiet except the cries of the hurting hearts they carried with them.

After a little while, we asked if they wanted to open up their one gift. They screamed, "Yes!" As each opened her gift, gratitude poured from the girls' lips. Right on cue, the first elf team came out, calling names of PCL girls. As the PCL girl responded with, "Here I am," a team of elves would come out with eighty gifts for her. One by one, each PCL girl was met by an elf with a gift train! It was a tender scene of beautiful chaos—screams, giggles, tears of joy, and Christmas wrap everywhere. I felt like I had given birth to fourteen girls, and I was a proud momma.

The wonder of this moment came as the girls began to open their gifts. They tore open the wrapping paper and saw the perfect gifts that were purchased for them. How could we know specific birthstones? How did we know that one of the girls loved Tinkerbell and collected all things Tink? We didn't know that, but God did. She got Tinkerbell pajamas and earrings, and all her gifts were wrapped in Tinkerbell paper. Over and over again, PCL girls opened their gifts and shouted, "How did you know?" We didn't—but God knew.

When it came time for me to give my talk, I realized that the message had already been shared. I love it when we are able to throw away our agendas and notes and go with the God flow of the moment. These young women are known by a God who loves them; they are completely known and completely loved. It was undeniable. They wholeheartedly agreed. Those girls began to attend church on Sundays, and a few eventually gave their lives to Christ—all to the glory of our great God!

This was a big, bold lesson in faith for me. When God nudges us into action, all we need to be is obedient. The results are up to Him. He will get the results He wants because He is doing it all. We did the inviting, but the Holy Spirit did the ministering. Each one of those girls walked away from that day with her arms full and her heart swirling with something she had never experienced before—being known and loved.

Bit of Brave

Is God nudging you today? Are you focused on the outcome instead of the obedient first step?

As we spend the next forty days together, we would do well to focus not on the outcome but the obedient first step.

Brave girl, you are known just like those PCL girls. God knows the first word you ever uttered on earth, and He already knows your last word. He knows you and loves you—every last messy part of you.

Let's take God at His word when He says in Jeremiah 29:13, "You will seek me and find me when you seek me with all your heart."

I don't know about you, but the thought of God being available to me just peppers my eggs. Let's seek Him over these next forty days and see what happens. Is that a deal?

This is what to expect over the next forty days. Each morning, we'll pray three things. (Listen, I'm not a morning person either, but let's take one for the team and meet together in the morning. It's forty days. Come on, you can do this!)

1. Pray daily for God to plant a seed of vision for your life.
2. Pray daily for the Holy Spirit to make you sensitive to see a need you can fill today.
3. Pray daily for the bravery to act upon that need.

It's hard to say what opportunities will be brought your way during the next forty days. You may find yourself being asked to love the unlovable in your life. Maybe God will spark a vision in your heart to care for a widow on your street. Maybe it's time to forgive your parent. Maybe God will show you areas that need some attention in order to be a better wife, mom, or daughter. I guarantee it will be out of your comfort zone.

You are probably reading this book because the status quo just isn't cutting it anymore. Are you tired of holding the hand of fear instead of faith? A lost world needs us to lay down fear and grab on tightly to faith. The world has been *told* a lot about Jesus. It's time to let God use our unlikely lives to *show* the world His Son.

At the end of each devotional, you'll find a bit of brave and room for you to journal your thoughts.

What's really exciting about this is that the brave girls you will meet over the next forty days are forty real women with the same fears that you and I share. They are forty ordinary, everyday women who know an extraordinary God. They'll share their stories of bravery and not-so-brave moments. You aren't alone. Let's do this together.

As you meet these women and hear their stories, I hope you see that we aren't very different from one another. We have more in common than you might think. We bleed when we're cut, cry when we're hurt, and we all need a Savior. Nobody has it all together, brave girl—nobody.

In addition to meeting during these forty days, I want to personally invite and encourage you to join the Brave Girl Boots group on Facebook. In the Brave Girl Boots group, you'll find a safe space to ask for prayer and be encouraged. I love what happens when women decide to look to one another with compassion instead of competition. You'll be met with buckets of grace and heaps of compassion in this online community. It's a judgment-free zone, I promise: *https://www.facebook.com/groups/bravegirlboots/*

Are you ready? I'll meet you in the morning, brave girl.

*Y*es! You showed up! I knew you would. Come in, and join us at the table. I want you to meet Anjeli Wilson, a wife, mom, and pediatrician living in Hendersonville, Tennessee.

Day One

If asked what I want most in life, my honest answer would probably be, "Control." I want to control what happens to me, how my day is scheduled, my kids' choices, and people in traffic. I especially want to control how people see me and what they think of me as well. Bravery for me is when I let go of that desire for control and choose to trust God completely.

One place where it seems easier for me to show courage is in Haiti, while helping to run small travel clinics in rural communities. Nothing there goes according to plan or schedule, and that's okay, because it forces me to rely fully on God rather than my illusion of control.

On the last day of my trip in March 2014, we had been told that clinic would have to be cancelled because the building we were to use was unavailable. Instead, we would go to an orphanage in the afternoon and do checkups on the fifty children there. After we arrived, we quickly saw that a steady stream of people from the community also began arriving at the orphanage to be seen. Among them was a woman in her sixties, struggling to breathe. She was unable to speak or even sit up.

After evaluating her, it was clear that she needed immediate treatment to save her life, and we didn't have the medication she needed. A search through our medication bags turned up a steroid that would take hours to work and another medication that might marginally improve her condition if it hadn't expired in 2009. We started an IV and decided to give her what we had, but I had little hope that she would survive. Then I heard the still, small voice of God nudging me to pray with her.

After a brief mental argument with God that this would only scare her, I put my brave girl boots on and hesitantly asked her if I could pray. She nodded. I don't remember much of what I prayed except that I asked God to supernaturally heal her. This is unlike me, as I really struggle with asking for God to physically heal someone. It's a control and self-protection thing. If I don't ask, then God can't hurt me by saying, "No." I forget that it also protects me from seeing Him say, *"Yes!"*

Within a minute of the end of the prayer, the woman began to speak in sentences, and within another minute, her lung exam was completely normal. I sat beside her and explained that God had given her a miracle. The medications we had given could not have worked that well in so little time. She began to talk excitedly, and I looked to the translator to explain. He told me the woman had been to church the day before and asked the elders to pray for her illness. After the service, one of them had told her, "Tomorrow, God is going to do a miracle for you." I was left absolutely speechless. When my agenda would have been for us to have the right medicine, His was to remind me that He alone is the Great Physician who can heal not only the body, but my control-seeking heart as well.

"O Lord my God, I cried to you for help, and you have healed me" (Psalm 30:2 ESV).

Bit of Brave In what area in your life are you tying God's hands by not trusting Him?

*G*ood morning, sweet brave girl! You came back. Yay! Today, I want you to meet Christa Alberts, a wife and mom living in Westland, Michigan. She is also our worship leader at CG events.

Day Two

I'm going to talk about the bravery it requires to hope. Hoping for something that has not yet come to pass requires bravery. In order to hope, you have to open yourself up to the possibility of disappointment and pain. That hurts. There are many people who decide to not hope for anything out of fear of being hurt.

As Christ-followers, we know our hope is in God. Hope, according to *Webster's Dictionary,* is to "expect with confidence that something will happen." So we are confident in God that He has our best interest in mind and that His plan is better than our own. We know this, don't we? But then fear of disappointment; being hurt, rejected, or forgotten; or pretty much anything can keep us from actually putting our trust in God and allowing ourselves to hope.

I have experienced this very thing. I trusted God but was afraid to hope at the same time. That sounds like a contradiction, right? I trust that God's plan is better than my own, but I also know my plans and hopes might not come to pass. These are things I want desperately!

My husband and I have been hoping for a child for almost five years now. Infertility and other medical issues have kept me from being able to conceive. We decided adoption was the direction we should go and really felt that God wanted us to adopt as well. We started our adoption journey almost four years ago. We are still waiting. I have had moments of confidence that what we hope for will happen, and I've also had moments when I'm afraid to hope. In this journey, we had a failed adoption and then years of waiting with no contact—no sign of anything. It is hard to hope, because what if the thing we hope for doesn't happen?

About ten months ago, my seven-year-old niece complained of a headache and lost consciousness. We rushed to the hospital, prayed for healing, and waited with great hope—or so I thought. As I sat in the hospital, praying and waiting, I was afraid to hope. Don't get me wrong—I *wanted* my niece to be okay. I wanted it to be over and for this bad dream to go away, but I had a hard time hoping. I thought to myself, *I will just prepare for the worst, and then it won't hurt as much.*

We've all heard the phrase "prepare for the worst; expect the best." Well, I only did the first part. I truly believed that if I hoped and expected with confidence that she would wake up and be okay, it would hurt all the more if she wasn't okay. I struggled with this the entire time we were in the hospital. Our worst fears did come to pass when our sweet Abby didn't wake up. She passed away, and guess what? Her death hurt just as much or more than I had prepared myself for. In the process, I didn't hope. I withdrew my trust in God and shut Him out. I didn't experience the peace that I might have had if I had put my hope in Him.

So why do I tell you all of this? I have learned through these experiences that hope requires bravery. It requires you to let your guard down and put yourself in situations where you might be disappointed or hurt. Even in situations where you have no other choice but to hope, it takes bravery to actually hope.

I have learned there is freedom in not only trusting that God is in control, but also hoping for things even if they might not come to pass. There is peace in knowing and expecting with confidence that God is there for me and has a plan.

If you find yourself in a place that requires hope, I pray you will step out with bravery. Anyone can *not* hope. Anyone can expect the worst or be pessimistic. Hope requires bravery. Hope also brings joy, peace, freedom, and closeness to our Father that you might not know otherwise.

I'll leave you with one of my favorite verses, Jeremiah 29:11: "'For I know the plans I have for you,' declares the Lord, 'plans to prosper you and not to harm you, plans to give you hope and a future.'"

Bit of Brave What have you closed your heart to hope for?

*G*ood morning! You are a champ! Good for you; you've made it to the third day! This morning at our table is Cassie Hull, a wife and mom living in Westland, Michigan.

Day Three

Bravery looks different in different people, and God recently showed me this. I thought that I wasn't brave. I haven't had to face any serious illnesses or health problems. I haven't faced job loss or severe financial problems. I haven't had to raise my kids on my own. I haven't done any high-adventure activities like skydiving or bungee jumping. People I know have been brave for those reasons, but not me. Yet I am brave in my own way. I had to step out of my comfort zone, face my insecurities, and change the way I was living.

I have been overweight for as long as I can remember. My weight has been a roller coaster over the years as I've gone through different periods of life that cause weight gain or loss as well as the occasional fad diet. But God got my attention early this year through a book called *Made to Crave* by Lysa TerKeurst. I have been an emotional eater in the worst way. I went to food for everything: happiness, sadness, boredom, anger, you name it. As a result of reading that book, God called me to stop turning to food for comfort and turn to Him instead. "You have circled this mountain long enough. Now turn north" (Deuteronomy 2:3 NASB).

This meant a lifestyle change. This wasn't another fad diet where I returned to my old eating habits after six months or so. I had to pull myself out of the rut I was stuck in and never go back. The author says, "God made us to consume food, not for food to consume us." But food had consumed me for so long that it was very hard to make the necessary lifestyle changes God called me to.

When I read Tami's message asking if I would write a post for the Brave Girl Boots challenge, I thought that I wasn't brave enough. I thought that I would answer Tami with a no, but I just didn't answer at first. Much to my surprise, God answered for me. When I went to the Lord in prayer, He told me, "You are being brave right now. You have just begun a journey that will change your whole life. That is being brave."

Made to Crave isn't about weight loss; it is about total dependence on God. I have surrendered the area of food to God, and I am trying my hardest to fully depend on Him. I want desperately to crave Him and not food. "You satisfy me more than the richest feast" (Psalm 63:5a NLT).

Bit of Brave What first step is God asking you to take?

The coffee is hot this morning, brave girl! I'm very glad you are here. I want you to meet another brave girl, Amy Sisco. Amy is a wife and mom residing in Garden City, Michigan.

Day Four

Finding Bravery amidst Brokenness

The biggest thing God is teaching me is that I'm an absolute mess. (It takes bravery to admit this.) I am learning much from an incredibly godly friend of mine who is a pastor's wife. She is a beautiful mess, too. She would tell you that herself. The most valuable lessons she has shared with me haven't come from a well-polished, put-together, proper Christian woman. I've learned the most from her not-looking-good, ugly-stuff moments!

I have learned from the times when my friend was broken and honest before God, when she screwed up or acted like a stubborn child. During those times, Jesus spoke sweetly into her heart and soul to come as she was. She is real and raw. It takes bravery to admit you are broken and be vulnerable. I believe a lie has permeated our Christian circles—that to be a good, godly woman who can lead others to Him, you have to have it all together, or at least look like you do.

I still get nervous inviting friends over when laundry overflows into my living room and there are so many things yet to be done to my house that it's almost ridiculous. But I still do. Those are some grace-filled times. I try my best to find my Mount of Olives amidst my Mount of Laundry and Mount of Dishes because Jesus is where it is at, gals. His Word is truth. This truth leads me to take off my mask that the world often pressures me to wear over my ugly, not-put-together self. Our friends, coworkers, and neighbors need more genuine, broken Christians who are not afraid to show some scars. They need the healer of broken things.

First-world problems can be quite discouraging. But we all suffer from them. Brave girls, we all have things in us that need fixing. Allowing God complete and utter access can be quite scary— which seems silly! He is God, after all. Growth is a process. We are made for more, and God is trustworthy and patient. He loves us so!

I'm a huge work in progress. I like to think I'm a masterpiece that takes a really long time because I keep flinching or questioning God's choice in paint color. But I am broken and handing all my shattered pieces over to Him so He can make something beautiful. Sharing our humanness with others will lead them to know Christ. That in itself is quite beautiful. "He heals up the brokenhearted and binds up their wounds" (Psalm 147:3).

Bit of Brave Are you withholding forgiveness from someone? Write a prayer today asking for God to give you insight in this situation.

Are you praying the following daily?

1. Pray daily for God to plant a seed of vision for your life.

2. Pray daily for the Holy Spirit to make you sensitive to see a need you can fill today.

3. Pray daily for the bravery to act upon this need.

*B*rave girl, I'm very proud of you for hanging in there with us! We love having you on this journey. As you pray, is God beginning to open your eyes to things you were previously blind to? I want you to meet Peg Cicci, a wife, mom, and grandma living in Macomb, Michigan.

Day Five

Have you ever had the occasion to be really brave? I hadn't until I received a cancer diagnosis with a prognosis that seemed very dire. I look back from the blessed perch of being healthy today. Was I brave as I went through the worst despair I have ever felt? No, I wasn't brave. I was a basket case—at least, I felt like one. I felt punched in the stomach; I lamented the future for my children without me. I wailed aloud when in my home alone. I came to the end of myself as I lay face-down on the floor, begging God to help me. No, I was not brave.

My family, friends, and everyone who loved me *were* brave. Despite their own worries about my future, cares, and priorities, they all put me first. They dropped everything and fervently prayed for me. They traveled with me for expert medical consultations and procedures, encouraged me, boosted my spirits, hugged me, and took care of my kids. They also cooked meals and were available by phone or text message whenever I needed reassurance.

Was I brave? I don't think I showed any courage, valor, or fearlessness at all. But I can say I had the nerve, daring boldness, and stoutheartedness to move through the situation with hands held by loved ones and eyes and hopes toward Heaven. Sometimes being brave isn't about being stoic or not needing any help; it's just about moving forward and not being paralyzed.

Psalm 116:6–7 says, "The LORD protects the unwary; when I was brought low, he saved me. Return to your rest, my soul, for the LORD has been good to you."

Bit of Brave Who do you need to be brave for today?

*O*h, brave girl! Are you getting a little bit stronger in your brave girl boots? We hope so! Don't give up. Keep meeting us in the morning. The coffee is good, and the company is even better. Stopping by this morning is Christy Perez, a wife and mom living in Clermont, Florida.

Day Six

When I think of bravery, I see the faces of my brother-in-law, his wife, and their two daughters who have just arrived here to the United States from their present-day, civil war-torn homeland.

They risked their lives. They packed three suitcases (leaving everything else behind) and slipped quietly into the dark, empty streets of their city. They walked for half an hour, praying all the while not to bump into the military or other criminals. They hired a taxi to drive them through back roads in the mountains, speeding past checkpoints, all to reach the neighboring country border and walk through like it was any normal day. The bravery that this required was insurmountable in my mind. Four flights and two days later, they arrived here to a home furnished completely with good-quality items by the family of God.

I have never before seen God literally open the floodgates of heaven and pour out His blessings and provision on someone like I saw during this family's journey. They sleep in peace tonight because they were willing to be brave. That same day, just hours after their escape, the border to their country was closed, and now none of their fellow citizens are able to leave.

If they hadn't been brave that morning for just a few hours, their lives would have taken a very different path than the one they see before them today. A moment of bravery can have a lifelong impact!

I realize this is an extreme situation, almost like an illusion. Our stories—my story, your story—might not require this same level of bravery, or maybe they do. There comes a time in each person's life when she or he has a choice to trust God or not to trust Him.

I've recently come through a season of not trusting God for the first time in my life. My family had gone through years of different types of losses, grief, and major stressors at the same time that my husband and I both went through periods of anxiety and depression. At some point, it felt like God was being intentionally hurtful. I became silent. I stopped hoping, praying, or worshipping.

It was an ugly, painful time. I eventually forgave God for the hurts that I felt. (Even though He doesn't need our forgiveness, my heart simply needed to forgive.) But I wasn't quite ready to be "all in" with Him again. About this time, a dear, sweet lifelong friend offered to fast and pray with me for a change in my spiritual state. This act of bravery and kindness completely shocked me, and I took her up on it. We agreed to fast and pray for two days.

I prayed without ceasing throughout those two days. I felt nothing. I sensed that the fast would be longer. I kept thinking it would last ten days, but that seemed long, so I just took it one day at a time. On the second day, I found out about the civil war in my family's home country and decided to continue the fast while praying over their safety. I woke each day and went to bed each night in fear for them.

All of the physical anxiety I had experienced before heightened; my heart pounded out of my chest for days on end. As the fast continued, I chose to seek God in the midst of that anxiety. God strengthened me to get through each day. One day, I began to see how He was miraculously protecting my family and at the same time providing for them here in the United States. I had a sense of peace that His provision here meant He would get my family to the US safely.

That same day, my sister-in-law e-mailed and told me that she was no longer afraid. She could see how God was providing for her family and protecting them. God gave her the same peace. That was on day ten. I broke my fast that day because my trust in God had been restored (which was the original reason for the fast). My family members were not stateside yet, but I trusted Him.

Today, I stand on the other side of the chasm. In those ten days, God took me from a place of brokenness in which I felt disenchanted with Him to a place where I trusted Him so fully that I did not fear when I knew my family was walking through the dark, war-torn streets with their suitcases. I have now watched the fulfillment of His protection and provision. I wish I had trusted Him more fully along the way. This experience was a great lesson for me.

If you are, or have ever been, in a place where you wondered whether you could trust God, know that you are not alone. Trusting Him sometimes requires bravery. There may be times when you don't receive the answer you were hoping for. Determined bravery is required to keep trusting Him.

In Deuteronomy 32:39, our Lord declares, "See now that I, even I, am he, and there is no god besides me … I wound and I heal" (ESV). Things don't always turn out like they did in this story. I experienced that multiple times during the past five years. You may have as well. I am beginning to see a glimmer of purpose in the heartache we experienced. When I doubted God the most, I always came back to the thought, *but Jesus.*

God isn't answering my prayer the way I want. Maybe He doesn't really hear me or love me, but Jesus … God has hung us out to dry; maybe we weren't good enough for Him. I want to give up, but Jesus … God seems to be purposefully crushing me, but Jesus … God (fill in the blank from your own story), but Jesus …

Jesus was brave for us when He went to the cross. When you feel like giving up over the next thirty-four days, remember Jesus. Now put on those brave girl boots for Jesus. When we are brave in God, we have the opportunity to see Him work in ways that we would not otherwise see. Let's go big in our bravery! "For though the Lord is high, he regards the lowly" (Psalm 138:6 ESV)

Bit of Brave Have you let fear come between you and God?

*G*ood morning, brave girl! I wonder what God is stirring inside your heart during this first week. You've hung in there for seven days—way to go! High-fives all around. I'm buying the hot beverages this morning. I insist! This morning, Lindsey Clifford is joining us. She is a wife and mom living in Whitmore Lake, Michigan. I think you'll like her. I'm sure you'll be friends.

Day Seven

The small things make us see the big picture. Just a few days ago, my friend stopped by my house after dark, close to 9:00 at night. She noticed that on my road, there was an elderly man walking alone. I live in a rural area outside of the city limits. The sight of a man walking late at night down our road was unusual. She stopped and asked him if he needed anything. He said, "No," and she went on her way. She shared this with me when she arrived at my house.

It occurred to me that he could possibly be a resident at the assisted living facility located across the street from me. My friend said she would call the police station on the way home. I considered getting in my car to check on him after she left. I thought about calling the sheriff's station myself. I contemplated calling the facility across the street. Instead, I did nothing. I assumed that someone else would do it.

The next morning, I woke to the sound of helicopters circling over my house. The elderly man was indeed a resident at the facility across the street. He had been gone all night.

I could have helped him, and I did *nothing*. I felt numb as I heard the helicopter go back and forth, searching for this lost man. I felt sick as I watched the news flashing his picture and showing the area close to my house where he disappeared. Twenty hours passed before authorities finally found the gentleman. He was found across the street from my home in a field where he had fallen. He was cold, dehydrated, and confused but alive—praise God! All I could think was, *I could have helped, but I did nothing.*

I don't ever want to have to say that again: "I could have helped, but I did nothing." I don't want to be numb to what God is calling me to do. I don't want to assume that someone else will do what I should do. I don't want to ignore those who are in need because there are so many in need. I don't want to lose my saltiness or my light.

Matthew 5:13–16 calls us to be the light of the world, to shine brightly and let others see our good deeds so that everyone will praise God! I encourage you to do what God is calling you to. Do it even if you think it may be a small task, something that someone else will do, or something you aren't comfortable doing. God delights in using us, even in things that we may think are small. You don't know when a small thing is actually a big thing. We never know when God will take a big thing and turn it into something huge.

Bit of Brave Is there something that God is nudging you to do? Are you resisting Him? Does it seem like a small thing?

*H*ello, beautiful brave girl! We're really doing this! Today, Sue Gentry shares her story of bravery. Sue is a mom and grandmother living in Romulus, Michigan. She isn't a coffee drinker, but we let her at our table. I know; I don't understand it, either—but we love all people, right?

Day Eight

Have you ever lost your child? No one does this intentionally, of course, but in the blink of an eye, that child is just *gone*. For those first frantic moments, you search through clothes racks or yell across the school yard. Over and over, you call your child's name, getting louder and louder as your fear escalates.

Where does every mother's thought pattern go? *If I don't find them right away, someone will take my child, and I'll never see them again.* Why do we automatically think that? We live in a sinful world, but we also know how valuable children are to us, so it's only natural to us that someone else would want them too! They are priceless people in our lives, and if they are lost, they take pieces of our hearts with them when they go.

Mary may have felt the same way. She was with Joseph, returning from her parental duty of dedicating Jesus at the temple, and all of a sudden, she realized Jesus was lost! (Luke 2:41–52) "How could I lose my own son?" she may have asked herself. (Don't worry, Mary; every mother has been there.) For *three days,* she could not find Him. Can you imagine her panic, fear, and hopelessness mounting as each hour passed?

I can more than imagine, because like Mary, I have experienced times when my children were lost—apart from God and out of my sight. We can't kid ourselves and say just because they're older it doesn't hurt as much, because it does. We have hopes and dreams for our valuable children, just like Mary did. Just like Mary, we will continue to search until we find them safe. Then, like Mary, we may be able to say, "I have treasured all these things in my heart" (Luke 2:51).

How could Mary treasure a lost child at a time like this? She *knew* that God's plan was at work in His life. She had confidence and trust in the One who would keep her child safe when she could not. Therefore, brave mothers, aunts, and sisters, we are called to do the same. Sometimes, these brave girl boots are made for walking, but many times, they're simply made for trusting.

> Never be afraid to trust an unknown
> future to a known God.
>
> —Corrie ten Boom

Bit of Brave Has life not turned out how you originally thought it would? Are you struggling to be brave in a situation you never wanted?

*B*rave girl, how are those boots? You're breaking them in nicely, I see. Allana Guidry will stop by today to share her story of bravery. I hope you are encouraged. Allana is a wife and mom living in Toledo, Ohio. Would you like more coffee?

Day Nine

Brave is not a word I would ever use to describe myself. Though many have told me in 2013 that I was brave, it was hard not seeing myself as who I was. Many do not know my struggle with fear and the panic attacks I have experienced endlessly since age twelve. I tried to hide them from everyone around me. It got so bad that by the time I was sixteen, I wasn't able to even pick up a ringing phone. I was extremely involved in church and other activities, but that was only because I had friends who were involved. By the time I was married, I had panic attacks while waiting at the bus stop for my son. I couldn't drive to the grocery store unless my husband was with me. It seemed as though fear completely ruled my life.

Little by little, God has chipped away this immense fear. It seems every moment is another stepping stone to push this fear away. A big moment was when I found out I was pregnant. I have gone through ten miscarriages. I had two before my daughter Samantha was born, one between Samantha and Chayla, and seven after Chayla. Every milestone was agonizing. My twelve-week appointment was one of the hardest moments. Most of the babies had passed away between twelve and fourteen weeks. Learning to trust God was not an easy road. I worried a lot! God blessed our family with Nisa Faith on December 16, 2012.

Nineteen days after giving birth to Nisa, I was diagnosed with leukemia. I spun from an all-time high to an all-time low within days. One thing I can say for sure is that God is faithful. Exodus 14:14 says, "The Lord will fight for you; you need only to be still." This Scripture has been my cornerstone. Stilling the fear that tries to attach itself to my heart is an endless battle.

I suppose being willing to fight against fear is brave. Trusting God's goodness and faithfulness is sometimes a very scary road. Bad things happen. There is much pain and hurt in this world. But I truly believe that when we start trusting God's great love for us, we find freedom during those moments. Stop looking at the waves around you, and focus on His eyes. He is always ready to catch you.

Bit of Brave Who is going through a storm right now? How can you encourage this person to be brave?

*B*rave girl, aren't you glad you didn't hit snooze today? Well, since we're becoming best friends, I'll share that I hit snooze a few times. But we made it! Good for you! Shawn Smith Lantz is with us this morning. Shawn is a wife and mom living in Franklin, Tennessee.

Day Ten

Can someone be brave and afraid at the same time? I know the answer to that question is a resounding *yes*. The bravest woman I know is my mother, Nancy. After losing all of her possessions in a house fire thirteen months earlier, my mom found herself on an airplane headed for the continent of Africa. She began a new life with my dad as a missionary in the Democratic Republic of Congo.

My mother had never wanted to become a missionary. Pregnant with her fourth child, Mom found herself flung into nineteenth-century living conditions on a remote bush mission station with limited electricity, no running water, and a six-hour drive to the nearest hospital. Long before the days of Facebook, Skype, or e-mail, news from home usually took between six weeks and six months to get through the mail system in Congo.

My mother faced isolation, as she could not communicate with the Congolese because of the language barrier. She cried every day out of loneliness and culture shock for the first two years of the four-year term we spent in Congo before our return to the United States for our first furlough. The enemy of her soul taunted her with the lie that to be a real missionary, she would have to lose one of her children to a snake bite or malaria!

Jesus calls us to be obedient in spite of our fears. In 2013, my parents celebrated thirty-five years of serving Christ in the Congo. My mother continually thanks Jesus for accepting her scared heart along with her many insecurities and letting her make an eternal impact through Him on a people she initially did not want to serve.

Instead of losing her children, as she had feared, all four of us and our spouses serve Jesus in our own lives. Jesus took her life—a woman who obeyed Him in the midst of her fears—and used it to give her a life story bigger than any dreams she had for herself!

Bravery is doing something even though you are scared! "The Lord God is my Strength, my personal bravery, and my invincible army; He makes my feet like hinds' feet and will make me to walk [not to stand still in terror, but to walk] and make [spiritual] progress upon my high places [of trouble, suffering, or responsibility]!" (Habakkuk 3:19 AMP)

Bit of Brave Are you willing to pray for God's will to be done in your life—and really mean it?

*G*ood morning, brave girl! This morning, you'll meet Nora Syracuse. She's pouring herself a cup of coffee and joining us. Nora is a mom to two grown sons and lives in Belleville, Michigan.

Day Eleven

Being a single parent since 1995 has been my bravest journey. As long as I can remember, I've always wanted to be married and have a family. In my early thirties, I married a man with four children, and I had my instant family. I loved those children. I was truly blessed. My marriage lasted seven years. Within those years, I gave birth to two sons. Looking back, I realize God was never part of my plans, which is why my marriage ended. After my marriage failed, I found myself totally alone, broken, hurting, and raising two small boys on my own. I was raised Catholic and learned about religion at a young age, but I needed more than religion.

One day, a coworker gave me a scripture: Proverbs 3:5–6. "Trust in the Lord with all your heart and lean not on your own understanding; in all your ways acknowledge him, and he will make your paths straight." I had never learned Scripture. This also came from a woman I wasn't very fond of. But it got my attention.

I had no idea what was next for me. I thought I was strong and tough, but I had no strength and two small boys who depended on me. My counselor suggested a church support group called Divorce Recovery. I had little support in my life, I felt totally alone, and my fear was growing, so I felt Divorce Recovery was my only option. The first day I walked in, I saw a few hundred men and women in attendance. I sure didn't feel relief; I felt panic that so many people were also going through divorce.

My decision to join Divorce Recovery changed my life. I dedicated my life to Christ for the first time. I didn't learn more about religion but about a relationship with Jesus Christ. I also learned that through pain, there is healing, and God never left me. I was trying to live my life on my own terms and was only messing things up.

The following years were not easy, but I had a purpose. Jesus Christ was my Savior, Redeemer, and one true desire. Once I put my trust in Him, He gave me strength. He would never leave or forsake me. Before I knew it, God was working with Christian people surrounding me, dropping His loving words of courage right into my hands. Not only did Christ bring me back into His loving arms, but I also learned to pray and listen to the Holy Spirit through the Bible.

As years passed, I was able to help others who struggled and hurt and reassure them that they are never alone. Today, I find myself not remarried. But if marriage is God's plan, I'll put on my brave girl boots and trust in Him the second time around. As for now, I have been blessed beyond my dreams, serving God diligently. He is my reward.

Both my sons are grown and doing very well, living their own lives. Being brave doesn't mean you have to go through life alone. Reach out your arms; there will be someone there to take your hand, walk beside you, and lift you up, girlfriend.

Lamentations 3:22–25 says,

> Because of the LORD's great love we are not consumed, for his compassions never fail. They are new every morning; great is your faithfulness. I say to myself, "The LORD is my portion; therefore I will wait for him." The LORD is good to those whose hope is in him, to the one who seeks him.

Bit of Brave If you've experienced a big disappointment in your life, are you willing to give all those feelings to God and move forward?

Are you praying the following daily?

1. Pray daily for God to plant a seed of vision for your life.

2. Pray daily for the Holy Spirit to make you sensitive to see a need you can fill today.

3. Pray daily for the bravery to act upon that need.

*S*tretch it out, brave girl! You are doing great! I feel what's needed this morning is more coffee. Pass your cup my way. Frances Barra will share her story of bravery with us. She's already at the table. Let's join her—pardon the glitter. Frances is a wife and mom living in Winter Garden, Florida.

Day Twelve

I tried to be an atheist; it would hurt so much less to not believe in a God who could do things but would not do them for me. All of my beliefs and the teachings I embraced seemed like an illusion. My heart, world, and dreams were now in a million jagged-edged pieces surrounding me.

The fight for my faith had begun, and I did not run to slay my giant like that young shepherd boy David. I did not say, "I am the Lord's servant; let it be done to me as you say" like Mary did. I was not brave. I wasn't even a little bit bold. I was broken. On the rare days when I wasn't numb, I was incredibly sad. For the first time in my life, I did not have an answer, and the answers others gave felt as empty as the promises I once held as truth.

But my God was brave and patient. He waited. He sat with me. I believe when I sobbed, He hurt too. Sometimes He was silent. Sometimes He spoke. But more than anything, He held my hand as we began to pick up the pieces. He never lost His trust in me even though I had lost my trust Him. He was personal and intimate. He gently helped me see who He truly is instead of who

I thought He should be. Together, we cleaned up the pieces. In the process, I relearned who He was. I am still learning who God is. I often think I have Him figured out, but I have no clue of the expanse of His character, love, or grace.

If your path feels like one that God created just to be cruel, I do not have a big truth that will make you triumphantly jump up and shout, "I'm gonna go and be brave right now!" I have learned that the place where people ask why God doesn't intervene is a very personal part of the relationship He desires with us, and one answer does not fit all. Is this not the simplistic complexity of God? He is the answer, yet He does not answer each of us the same way. Through trials, we learn to know God and then trust Him. With this combination, we will be brave no matter what is given or taken away.

If you aren't in this place, but someone you love is, be patient. Prayer and patience are the best gifts you can give someone in the wake of brokenness. When there is nothing you can do or give to fix them, then bravely trust God with the process. As Helen Keller said, "We could never learn to be brave and patient if there were only joy in the world."

"Trust God from the bottom of your heart; don't try to figure out everything on your own. Listen for God's voice in everything you do, everywhere you go; He's the One Who will keep you on track. Don't assume that you know it all" (Proverbs 3:5–6 MSG).

Bit of Brave Who do you need to give the gift of patience and prayer to?

*B*rave girl Jaimee Forsyth is joining the party this morning. Jaimee is a single twenty-something living in Westland, Michigan.

Day Thirteen

Hi. I'm Jaimee, and I am a comparer.

I want to share about a struggle that I face almost daily: a battle with self-image. There are some days when I wake up, look in the mirror, and say, "Yes! Lord, You did great!" But in a more realistic scenario, I am prone to beat myself down. I look at myself, look at the person next to me, and decide that I just don't measure up.

Whether in the area of looks, biblical knowledge, worship leading, attention received from men, or being a good leader, it's very easy to compare yourself to others and put yourself down. You may even begin to feel worthless.

God began to show me something while I was away on a youth retreat: we need to be brave enough to accept that God made us to be who we are! There is no comparison in God's eyes between you and other believers. We are all His children, and we are all made with different gifts, talents, and beauty! Each and every one of us brings something meaningful, and He will use us in our own unique ways if we just believe He will!

We have great worth in the Lord. *You* have great worth. I know it's time for me to truly start believing in this truth!

"You're blessed when you're content with just who you are—no more, no less" (Matthew 5:5a MSG).

Bit of Brave Who are you comparing yourself to—and why?

*C*arrie Stanley is in the kitchen this morning! She is as bold for Jesus as her hair color. You'll be friends with her in no time. Carrie is a wife and mom living in Garden City, Michigan.

Day Fourteen

Brave is a verb that means "to endure or face unpleasant conditions or behavior without showing fear" (*Webster's* definition).

I was the poster child for perfect Sunday school attendance. I have sang and served in church for as long as I can remember, and I gave my whole heart to Jesus when I was ten years old. This, of course, would mean that I have spent most of my life growing in my faith. I had faced obstacles—or "unpleasant conditions," as *Webster's* calls them—many times and put on a brave face masked behind my faith in God. Don't get me wrong; I had faith, but my faith was a mix of trust in Christ and the control I thought I had over the obstacles.

This breed of faith was put to the test in August 2009 when my daughter was diagnosed with an aggressive cancer called neuroblastoma. She was only eighteen months old and the third of my four children. My husband was in college and working an odd mix of three part-time jobs. He had to quit two of them during our war on cancer. The next nine months were filled with chemo, surgery, lots of hospital stays, and more life and faith lessons than I ever thought possible in such a small amount of time. By May 2010, my husband and I were told there was nothing left for the doctors to try and that Leiryn had two to three months left.

It is now 2015, and my daughter is still alive—talk about a miracle. I am forever grateful for the time that we've had, but it has been exceptionally difficult living in limbo. Imagine yourself sitting in front of the Hoover Dam without the dam, and the water is just sitting there. It's a miracle, and you have to appreciate that for what it is—but you also have no control over when all of that water will come crashing down. This is our life. We are forever waiting for the water to come crashing down.

I've been told countless times how brave I am and how there's no way another would be able to do what I'm doing. Others say their faith isn't as strong as mine. But I've learned that there's a fine line that often gets blurred between the *Webster's* definition of bravery and having faith in what God is doing through the unpleasant situation—not just for others, but for your relationship with Him. To me, being brave isn't something that comes from within yourself; it's admitting in the midst of the storm that you don't have anything to offer without God.

Bit of Brave What fuels your fears today? List three words.

Are you praying the following daily?

1. Pray daily for God to plant a seed of vision for your life.

2. Pray daily for the Holy Spirit to make you sensitive to see a need you can fill today.

3. Pray daily for the bravery to act upon this need.

*B*rave girl, we have two weeks in. Good job! This morning, you'll meet my pastor's wife, Nancy Barra. She loves Jesus and coffee. We're in good hands. Nancy is a wife, mom, and grandmother in Canton, Michigan.

Day Fifteen

I have loved being in full-time ministry with Rocky for most of our forty-two years of marriage. We have an awesome church and many wonderful friends. The most important part of my Christian journey is not the work I do for God and others. I know that it's the intimacy of my relationship with Him. An intimate relationship with God requires daily intentionality, time in His Word, and surrender in prayer.

My life is busy, and the battle often starts with spending time with God—really surrendering my day to Him and asking Him to fill me with His Holy Spirit. If I don't spend time with Him, forget the brave girl boots. I won't need them. I'll be doing my thing—not bad stuff, just not what makes a difference for eternity.

It's not always simple to do what we're being challenged to do these forty days. The first challenge is easy. Pray for God to plant a seed of vision for your life. That's awesome! Then, pray that the Holy Spirit will give you the sensitivity to see a need you can fill that day. Again, that's a wonderful prayer, and I believe that He will show us needs. There's plenty out there. Now, pray for the bravery to act upon that need.

It's not that hard for most of us to pick up meals. (It may be carry-out. I don't cook much!) We can drop cards in the mail, make phone calls, send texts or e-mails, or hug and pray with someone at church who needs encouragement. Those are all passions of mine, and I believe that God uses all of those gestures. No brave boots are needed, though. I love to do those things; they're totally in my comfort zone.

God orders our steps. The people He puts next to me on planes; waiting with me in offices; in the line at stores, banks, or businesses; and others in my neighborhood often have purpose. God has put us together there for a reason—sometimes to talk about Him and sometimes not to. But I ought to always represent Him well. I want the presence of Jesus to be seen in my life, coming through to others. I want others to see Jesus, not Nancy—not who I am myself, but who I am in Christ. I want others to see Jesus in and through me.

This is why my brave girl boots are required every day. I want the day-to-day purpose and plans for my life to be His plans. I want to be brave enough to open my mouth and share the Good News with whoever God wants me to. This is my prayer: "Pray also for me, that whenever I open my mouth, words may be given me so that I will fearlessly make known the mystery of the Gospel" (Ephesians 6:22).

Bit of Brave Who is the last person you shared the gospel with? If you can't remember, take heart. Today is a new day. Are you willing to pray for God to open up a door to share His love? Write your prayer in the space below.

*B*rave girl, a boy momma is in the house today. I want you to meet Melissa Mulvaney. She is a wife and mom living in Canton, Michigan.

Day Sixteen

We watch movies about being brave and sing songs about it. But are we brave?

Recently, I really believed that God was preparing me to be brave—life-altering, no-looking-back brave. Everything I read, every song heard, all my Bible study topics, the Scriptures I was e-mailed each morning—they all pointed to me needing to get prepared for being really brave. I wish I could tell you that I was completely, utterly, "Come at me, Satan" brave. But I wasn't.

I had moments when I would cry out to God. I begged. I wept the only words that would come out: "Please, God; don't make me have to be this brave. Please." But when the tears stopped—when I stopped—I took a breath and felt it. I felt confident that if He did, in His divine providence, decide to have me walk through this door, I could be brave. But only the fact that He that lives in me would make me brave.

The peace that washed over me was almost intoxicating. Knowing that I would not be alone, that Christ had been through that door before was enough. I knew He would not leave or forsake me. He would put my brave girl boots on me Himself and walk through the valley with me. Would I have had support from family and friends? Absolutely. Undoubtedly. But knowing that my Savior would walk with me, hold me, and never leave me was enough to make me brave.

And maybe that's all God needed to teach me this time. In His amazing grace, He closed the door and locked it. I wept. I uttered, "Thank you, thank you, thank you" until I couldn't anymore. I think it was enough. In this moment, it was enough for my Lord to know that I would've depended on Him as my source of hope, grace, and peace. I already depend on Him. But there is nothing like standing in a doorway with shaking hands and feet, trying to pull on those brave girl boots, and knowing that He would put those boots on with His nail-torn hands Himself.

I pray that wherever you are right now—in a valley, on a mountaintop, waiting in the hallway, or with knocking knees in a doorway—you will discover that Christ is enough. That truth will not just make you brave, but also set you free. "Finally, be strong in the Lord and in the strength of his might" (Ephesians 6:10 ESV).

Bit of Brave Are you living like God is not enough?

*G*ood morning, brave girl! You are doing great on this journey. I am very thankful for you. Iris Ramirez is with us this morning. Iris is a wife and mom living in Earth, Texas.

Day Seventeen

Many people think that being brave is synonymous with being fearless and untouchable. But for me, being brave has meant being vulnerable enough to admit my fears and weaknesses. It also means leaning on Jesus for strength and power to face and overcome them. This is a daily practice.

One of my greatest struggles has been my journey to health. About three years ago, God revealed to me that I was to help others honor Him with their bodies through strategic exercise, proper nutrition, and spiritual edification. He gave me the name Foundations 6:19, and ever since, I've poured endless energy and resources into fulfilling this calling. God has called me to encourage and equip others to be healthy for the purpose of honoring God with their bodies. Based on 1 Corinthians 6:19-20, we believe our bodies are God's temple. We gather for group fitness sessions weekly to focus on strategic exercise, proper nutrition, accountability and spiritual edification. I've enjoyed every minute of it, and I've learned much for my own benefit as well.

What does this have to do with being brave? Over the last few months, I have found myself ten pounds heavier and not quite sure when it happened. I know factors that contributed to it, but I don't know how I missed it happening. So my brave moment comes in admitting that even though I am a fitness professional, this does not make me any less human. That doesn't mean I have it all figured out. I still have struggles, but I know that I can face each one with a brave heart because God is still with me.

I can trust God to empower me to get back on track, learn from this, and use it as a way to encourage and equip others on their journeys. Being healthy isn't easy. It requires me to put on brave girl boots and make healthy choices. I do this not just to reach my own goals, but also to honor God with my body so that I can fulfill His purpose and plan for my life.

I want to encourage you if you fear getting healthy and what it's going to take to make changes and get results. Be of good courage, and be brave! Trust God to help you face your fears and overcome them—to honor God with your body and your whole life, one day, one choice at a time! "Do you not know that your body is the temple of the Holy Spirit, who is in you, whom you have received from God? You are not your own; you were bought at a price. Therefore honor God with your body" (1 Corinthians 6:19–20).

Bit of Brave How is your health? If you could be brave enough to make one change today, what would it be?

*B*rave girl, are those boots getting a bit worn? I'm very thankful we're in this together. You'll be glad you came for coffee this morning, because Heather Costa is sharing her story of courage. Heather is a twenty-something living in Wayne, Michigan.

Day Eighteen

I used to believe two things. First, I thought that my testimony and story were boring. I believed God was real, and I knew He had plans for my life. That's what I was taught growing up. I knew He loved me and had my best interests at heart, but I questioned how God would use me. My story seemed plain and boring.

I grew up in a Christian family, and Jesus had been the center of my world for as long as I could remember. Of course, I had times when I strayed from Him, times when I didn't trust or felt distant. But I knew He loved me despite my sin, despite how many times I messed up. I believed it in my head, but it sometimes took my heart a few beats to catch up. Still, I graduated high school knowing Jesus was all I needed.

I struggled with self-worth for a while, but in college, God gave me a moment when I knew without a shadow of a doubt that I was beautiful. More than that, I realized my worth came from Jesus alone. My identity was found in Him, not the things of this world that come and go and are measured by others' opinions.

As I continued through my college years, I met and fell in love with my husband. Jordan and I spent a year getting to know each other, four months dating, and thirteen months planning our wedding and enjoying all life had for us. Our wedding day was beautiful and greater than anything I could have ever imagined.

As the day came to a close, we started our trek to our honeymoon, stopping overnight somewhere in Ohio. As we started our drive the next morning, the unthinkable happened. The second thing I believed was that I was invincible. Bad things don't happen to people like me. I wish that were true, but it's not. *En route* to our honeymoon, the car we were traveling in flipped, and Jordan's very short life ended.

I was left widowed, not even twenty-four hours after I was married. As I sit suspended in air, on a flight back home from visiting my in-laws, there is much I could tell you about what God has done in my life. I wish I had the room to explain it all, but the most important thing for you to know is this: I know that God hasn't given up on me. He has seen me through the toughest of times and has guided me through the unthinkable.

When I didn't know what to do, I was given two choices: give up or push through. I'm a fighter, so every day, I choose to push through. I choose to hold on to Lamentations 3:22-23, "Because of the LORD's great love, we are not consumed, for his compassions never fail. They are new every morning; great is your faithfulness." I choose to move forward in life, not knowing what tomorrow brings.

I don't know what God has planned for me, but I know it's worth pushing through for. I'm reminded each day to choose life, to choose to live for my Savior. I know that He's right next to me with each breath and step that I take. "And we know that in all things God works for the good of those who love him, who have been called according to his purpose" (Romans 8:28).

Bit of Brave In what area of your life do you need to choose Jesus over your feelings?

Are you praying the following daily?

1. Pray daily for God to plant a seed of vision for your life.

2. Pray daily for the Holy Spirit to make you sensitive to a need you can fill today.

3. Pray daily for the bravery to act upon that need.

*B*rave girl, the house is a hot mess today. Walk over that pile of clothes, and come to the table. The coffee is hot, and Katy Reitz brought flavored cream! Katy is a wife and mom living in New Boston, Michigan.

Day Nineteen

Have you ever looked back at where you came from and were astounded at the distance your soul covered? While you trudged the distance, perhaps it felt like you only took baby steps that really wouldn't amount to anything ever.

I have felt this way. Often, I let out a big sigh and ask God, "Where am I going?" I wonder if He's really going to take me to the place where I feel I am headed.

In 2009, I was a stay-at-home mom with two young kids. I wanted to sew an apron; they were all the rage. I bought a pattern for $2.99 and fabric that caught my eye. Its print was bold black, red, and orange flowers. I had scant prior experience and no knowledge of how to really run my sewing machine. My mother had insisted I buy it in 2000 with my birthday money, but I pressed forward without any fear of what was ahead of me.

A couple hours later, I hopped on my iMac, took a quick picture with the camera, and posted a really bad photo of myself wearing the apron on Facebook. Comments came in, and friends wanted to purchase one! That wasn't my intention at all when I posted it. But it happened anyway. I started taking orders and selling aprons.

Fast-forward through many hours of sewing and searching for the right fabric for multiple custom orders, a few craft shows, and a Facebook fan page, and lil' alice was born. lil' alice is a handmade shop that began as a hobby and slowly transformed into a business. I have always been a creative person, even as a child. To have this creative outlet as an adult was a way for me to wind down after a long day as a stay-at-home mom. It allowed me to relax and focus on my creativity.

I found myself in constant prayer about what to do next with this accidental hobby. My husband, Rich, noticed that I was taking over his man cave above the garage, and my fabric stash was growing. My passion for this hobby wasn't going away quickly. Rich was supportive of my hobby and wanted it to stay just that—a hobby. But many times in my new sewing room that he made for me in the basement, I found myself begging God for clear direction. I needed answers, but I didn't know how I would know for sure when the time was right to make this hobby a business.

Then one September evening over dinner, the kids had left the table to go play. Rich and I lingered longer. He simply said to me, "Do whatever you have to do to make lil' alice a business!" It was that simple. I never had to state my case, beg, or convince. I simply prayed.

But I was scared out of my blasted mind! How would I make my hobby a business? How would I trademark my name? Even though I was scared, I prayed for wisdom with each step of the process.

lil' alice is constantly growing. I bring new ideas to the table, and the business is stretching me so far that I am afraid. I believe it's a healthy fear, but it requires me to do things beyond what I am capable of doing. I daily lean on God for wisdom to guide me to the next step. I take a glance back at where I have come since 2009 and am simply amazed! "If any of you lacks wisdom, he should ask God, who gives generously to all without finding fault, and it will be given to him" (James 1:5).

Bit of Brave Remember that dream of yours—the one covered in fear dust? Tell me about it.

ood morning, brave girl! Come here and hug me. We are halfway there! High fives! I'm very proud of you. My friend Laura Bayus is here sharing this morning. You'll like her. She's pretty awesome.

Day Twenty

Brave? Yeah, I've been brave all my life. It was always easy for me, because I grew up knowing a God who had my back. Who wouldn't be brave when they know the Creator of the universe is on their side? Well, in 2010, God began teaching me a new lesson in bravery and trust that proved to be one of the hardest, ugliest, most painful lessons of my life.

The challenge started during my pregnancy with our fourth child, when I began spotting at about fourteen weeks. Despite the reassurance by my doctor that these things do happen in normal pregnancies, I was admitted to the hospital within a few days when things got worse. "No fluid surrounding the baby" was the report the next morning, and the calm and trusting approach we had taken was instantly replaced with a can't-catch-my-breath fear.

No water for a fetus means impaired development at best. We were told that our baby wouldn't make it, and if by some miracle she did live, she would be severely physically impaired and/or mentally disabled. After the shock had worn off, Steve and I decided to be brave and trust that God would rescue us. So we hoped, and we prayed.

During the weeks of bed rest that followed, God made His presence known. It felt as though He was incredibly close, showing us and others signs that seemed to say, "I'm here. I know what you need. You can trust me." I believed beyond the shadow of a doubt that God would give us a miracle in this little one. Looking back, though, I believe God wanted to teach us a deeper meaning of trust.

I'm still reduced to tears (four years later) when I remember the events of September 17, 2010. Riding high on our faith, we patiently awaited God's rescue. Lying on the couch, asking for prayer from friends online, I was caught off guard by contractions—three within thirty minutes. This wasn't good.

My husband and I rushed to the hospital in complete shock and confusion when it became apparent that our baby was coming. Within an hour, I delivered my lifeless baby girl amid sobs and wails—ours and those of the hospital staff. The rain outside my hospital room fell as steadily as my tears in the torturous hours before I was finally discharged. I remember thinking how poetic it was—as if all of heaven wept with us. By then, however, I wasn't sure there even was a heaven or a God to share my grief.

My opinion of God became darker in the months that followed as I relived the events of that night in my mind. I couldn't help but think about the cruelty we'd endured. Rather than leaving the hospital with our precious baby girl in our arms, we brought her ashes home in a box. How could a loving God—a Father, no less—force His children to suffer like this?

If this was a test of my faith, I failed miserably. Instead of trusting the God I'd served all my life, I denied His existence. Still, verses of Scripture that I'd memorized in the past kept coming back to me. They

51

seemed to answer the doubt with reassurance of who God is, and I found that I couldn't be an atheist. But if there was an all-powerful God, I decided, He must not be kind and good like I'd once believed.

I decided that God must have created life on earth merely for His amusement. Our struggles and pains were nothing more than juicy plot twists in His favorite movie. But that belief didn't last long either. It seemed like every time I found myself wallowing in my sorrow and mentally rehashing my pain, I thought about how broken I was at the hand of the almighty voyeur, as I'd dubbed Him. Then one of my kids would randomly wander through the room singing his or her favorite TobyMac song. I'd be in deep, desperate thought, and then I'd hear, "This is love calling out to the broken ..." God reassured me of His love even as I denied Him!

I realize now that my heavenly Father never left my side as I walked through the fire of my loss. Looking back, I can see that the signs weren't His way of telling me everything would be okay. Rather, they encouraged me to keep believing in Him when things seemed like they couldn't get any worse. Often, God's encouragement to be brave comes right before disaster strikes, as if to say, "This isn't gonna look good. Trust me anyway."

It took years for my heart to fully heal and for me to be able to trust God again. But now, when He asks me to be brave, I'm able to do so. Even if things don't unfold the way I think they should, I know that my God—my good and loving Heavenly Father— has a plan to use my life, good times and bad, to write His story, and that in the end, it will be a beautiful thing. "Though he slay me, yet will I hope in him" (Job 13:15).

Bit of Brave Who came to your mind while reading today's devotional? Send that person a note of encouragement today. Do it now, before you forget.

*ood morning! Oh, yawn. How are you doing? I trust that God is meeting you each morning. He is good like that! Trish Kingsnorth is in the kitchen today, cooking up some kind of wonderful. I hope you brought your appetite. Trish is a wife living in Ypsilanti, Michigan.

Day Twenty-One

Me, brave? Has that question ever gone through your mind? It's crossed mine. It's interesting how we can convince ourselves that we are brave (for the most part) until our bravery is put to the test and we see what we are really made of. We find out if we are the brave daughters that God created us to be or more like the Cowardly Lion from *The Wizard of Oz*.

Over the past few months, I have experienced situations that I never faced before. I have to admit that the brave girl I imagined I was turned out to be more like the Cowardly Lion. The good news is that I shared my struggles with some other brave girls who helped remind me that I had the heart of a lioness, and I just needed to take that first step forward, put my brave girl boots on, and keep steppin'. They showed me that God was right there, leading the way through the situation even if I could not see the path He was leading me down.

At times, I did not understand the reason for the path I was on. But recently, I had an opportunity to meet a need of someone from my extended family. This was something that I would never have had the opportunity to do had I not been on this road.

I am walking out this transformation every day. I remind myself that God does have this well in hand. I know that nothing has taken Him by surprise and that my job is to listen closely, lean in, and look forward. Take this one thought for the day: don't be afraid to share your struggles. We all need to be reminded at times that we are braver than we realize. Keep looking forward, because that is where the light is shining, and that light will guide the next step you are to take. Do it in brave girl boots! "Your Word is a Lamp to my feet and a Light to my path" (Psalm 119:105 NASB).

Bit of Brave Are you learning to recognize the lie buried in your fear?

*G*ood morning, brave girl! Cassie Rea is at our table this morning. She is young, but don't let that fool you. I learn from her all the time. Cassie is a single twenty-something living in New Haven, Michigan.

Day Twenty-Two

Brave is not something I consider myself to be in the least bit. I'm not one to voluntarily do something outside of my comfort zone. I'm thankful that I serve a God who doesn't give up on me despite my lack of courage when it comes to doing His work.

In the summer of 2012, I had just graduated from high school. I really had no idea what I was going to do in the next season in my life, and I was scared. I looked to God for direction and didn't find anything. I knew what I enjoyed doing, but I wasn't sure where God wanted me to be. I had just finished an internship under my youth pastor, and I didn't know where I would go next.

I was in a season of waiting and searching. I had no idea where God wanted me to go next, and that was completely terrifying. I spent days just asking God for some sort of guidance. I had no idea what to do, so I started attending at the local community college and began working as a teacher's assistant. Although I loved what I was doing, it didn't feel right. I felt as if I was just filling the gaps to make it look like I was going somewhere. I knew God had something in store for me, but I had no idea what to look for.

It was insane how God came to me one day. It was the last thing I expected to happen. I was hanging out one night with my friend and pastor, Bryan. He told me that God had placed a vision for a church on his heart, and he wanted me to be a part of it. My mind raced with all of the details, but there was great peace in my heart about this decision. God had answered my calls. In seeking Him, I found where I needed to go.

I spent days and nights praying over this. That peace was so strong in my heart that I just knew this was my next step. I was extremely clueless as to how this all would work, not to mention incredibly nervous. I was also slightly doubtful of my ability to drop everything and gain full responsibility at eighteen. But over the next few months, I figured out my living situation, found a job, and began the process of moving out of my parents' house and closer to where the church would be planted.

I was terrified, but it was time for me to put on my brave girl boots and move on to the next part of my life.

So I went, and that was the best decision of my life. Despite my fear of the unknown, I put on my brave girl boots and followed where God called me to go—and I haven't looked back since. Through the waiting and the biggest transition of my life, I had my brave girl boots on, and I am so thankful I did. If I hadn't put them on and marched forward, I don't know where I would be today. "I pray to GOD—my life a prayer— and wait for what He'll say and do. My life's on the line before God, my Lord, waiting and watching till morning, waiting and watching till morning" (Psalm 130:5–6 MSG).

Bit of Brave Are you struggling with fear of the unknown? In what area do you struggle?

ood morning, brave girl! Are you catching on to the idea that you aren't alone on this road to bravery? We all struggle with you. Ami McCain, a single woman living in Redford, Michigan, joins us today.

Day Twenty-Three

A few days from now, a dream of mine will be laid to rest, and the death of this dream has me feeling anything but brave.

Eleven years ago, the Lord took my lost self and set me on a new path. As I experienced life for the first time, my dream—my holy obsession—first formed. I knew then that I wanted to work in a local church and share the same love I received with all who entered its doors.

Two years ago, that dream became a reality—and it's been nothing like I ever imagined. Having a front-row seat to see the Lord move is a treasured experience I wouldn't trade for the world. Supernatural provision, the answering of numerous prayers, watching people accept Christ as Savior week after week—these joys have been my norm. Yet there are shadows to this dream—ones that were unexpected and have slowly sucked the life and bravery right out of me. Many truths I held to be black and white have transformed into murky grays. This has caused me to introspectively challenge my faith, principles, and integrity.

Eighteen months into living this dream, my notoriously tender heart started hardening in order to meet the demands of reality.

That was when I first felt the Lord prompting me to take a brave step: allow this dream to die, or watch my heart die instead.

I believe it is the Lord who plants dreams in our hearts. He has specific purposes for each of us, and through those seeds of desire, He inspires us to take action. But God-given dreams that grow beyond God-given boundaries lead to idols of the heart. Soon we find ourselves worshiping created things more than the Creator Himself.

In God's tenderness, I've been reminded how He cherishes my heart first and foremost. "I will give you a new heart and put a new spirit in you; I will remove from you your heart of stone and give you a heart of flesh" (Ezekiel 36:26). What a promise! Proverbs 4:23 tells us to "Watch over your heart with all diligence, for from it flow the springs of life" (NASB). Life flows from a heart guarded against disruption from worship of its Creator, and *anything* includes God-given dreams.

While painful and unnatural, I'm choosing to put my dream to death in order to experience life. Anyone who's ever had a dream die can relate to the sadness this brings. But before there can be any resurrection, we must first encounter death. God's proven Himself to be the One who's brave, so we know with confidence that we can "hold unswervingly to the hope we profess, for he who promised is faithful" (Hebrews 10:23).

Bit of Brave Is God whispering to you about a new season He wants to bring you into? What do you need to lay down in order to follow where God leads?

*G*ood morning, brave girl! Do you hear that singing in the kitchen? That's Dalina Stephens. She's joining us this morning. Dalina is a wife and mom living in Canton, Michigan.

Day Twenty-Four

> Sing to God, sing praise to his name, extol
> him who rides on the clouds - his name is
> the Lord - and rejoice before him. A father to
> the fatherless, defender of widows is God in
> his holy dwelling!
>
> —Psalm 68:4–5

My life is one of many ups and downs.

After being taken advantage of several times by multiple people in my adolescent years, I found myself single with three kids at age twenty-three. I was running from God and any pure love. When baby number three came along and his father wanted to marry me, this was my chance to make my life right. He had a good job, and I would have been financially secure for the rest of my life. But God had a different plan.

My mom invited me to a ladies' conference. During the prayer time, the worship team started singing,

> It's hard to understand when life seems unfair,
> you're carrying this load that you're not meant
> to bear. He said in His Word that peace could be

found if you will just find the courage to lay it all down. At Your feet, at Your feet, I humbly bow before You; with honor, I adore You. At Your feet, at Your feet, there is no place I'd rather be than at Your feet.

I think I knocked the lady next to me down getting to the altar— and I did just what the song said. After this experience, I was never the same. I started praying, reading the Word, and attending every church service I could find. I tried my best to focus on what the Lord wanted in my life instead of what I wanted.

Through this time, God showed me that I didn't need to get the love and approval of a man. The love I needed came only from God. His healing began. I realized that I needed to please God and be happy with who He made me to be. Once I really began to love what God had created in me, I was able to receive His love in a greater way.

God was the one who loved me and would care for me the way I needed. He gave me the courage I needed to live life abundantly. Over a six-year span, I released all things to Him, and He has fulfilled me in every way possible. I am now married to a wonderful man, and we are taking care of our six children. My life has become something beautiful to God and me.

My encouragement to you is this: if you allow God to be your first source of love, you will be completely fulfilled.

Bit of Brave Do you think you are too far from God to take a step toward Him?

*B*rave girl, have I told you lately how proud I am of you? Meeting in the morning is no small feat. You are awesome. I like you. Tracey Solomon is bringing the brew this morning. Can you smell that fresh-ground goodness? Tracey is a wife and mom living in Canton, Michigan.

Day Twenty-Five

A year ago, the ambulance first pulled up to our neighbor's house. Nosy—I mean, caring—as I am, I found out that our neighbor of thirteen years was battling pancreatic cancer. We prayed for our neighbor and frequently asked how he was doing as we battled our own health challenges. (My husband has advanced prostate cancer.) I hate cancer, and I'm pretty sure Jesus does too.

A few weeks ago, the ambulance made another early morning visit. The next day, my neighbor's driveway overflowed with cars in the middle of a weekday. That can only mean one of two things: either there was a new baby, or our neighbor had lost his battle. There was no new baby.

Heartbroken for their loss, I desperately wanted to do something to help. But there was a dilemma. (Or rather, a complication.) Our neighbors are Muslim. I know what to do for most friends who suffer a loss. I go, sit, cry, listen, and (Italian momma that I am) I bring food. Due to our different beliefs, most of my go-to ways to love and help went out the window. Muslims have dietary rules that mean the nice Italian lady next door can't really cook for them. My kitchen is not halal (the Muslim equivalent of Kosher).

I'll be honest—I was intimidated, overwhelmed, and afraid. I didn't know how to help.

I prayed, "Lord, I don't know the rules! I don't want to offend! But Your Word says to love my neighbor, and my neighbors are Muslim, so I'm going to need some help figuring out how to do this." Then I remembered the halal grocery near our home. If I couldn't cook, at least I could go buy some prepared goodies and make a care package. That was an adventure in itself. I don't know the difference between Indian and halal food, but the owner graciously helped me. I also offered our driveway for parking and shared the salt we had to help clear their walks. (This was during the great salt shortage of 2014.)

After delivering the goodies, I still wondered if I'd done enough or too much. Later, there was a quiet knock on my front door. It was the neighbor's grandson, holding a plate of warm food—for us. He wanted to thank us for the salt, parking, and care package by bringing a plate from the funeral dinner. In their pain, they thought tenderly of us. How amazing is that? Apparently, my gift hadn't offended. My small, outside-the-box actions had spoken love. Thank you, Jesus.

Sometimes being brave means loving outside the box. People who are different are a little more complicated to love. Today, I pray that we each find ways to love our neighbors, regardless of our differences. I'm pretty sure Jesus takes delight when we do.

> Jesus replied: "Love the Lord your God with all your heart and with all your soul and with all your mind. This is the first and greatest commandment. And the second is like it: 'Love your neighbor as

yourself.' All the Law and the Prophets hang on these two commandments." (Matthew 22:37–40)

Bit of Brave Is God nudging you to be brave enough to love someone in a way that is outside the box?

ello, brave girl! We've been best friends for twenty-six days now! Please just walk in my home; there's no need to ring the bell. You always have a place at my table. Joining us this morning is Tamara Gissendaner. She is all kinds of awesome. You'll love her! Tamara is a wife and mom living in Superior Township, Michigan.

Day Twenty-Six

I've always struggled with an ugly case of perfectionism. When allowed to, it keeps me from being productive. It's the subconscious notion that if I can't do something perfectly, I won't do it at all.

By age twenty-six I was a married stay-at-home mom with four children. When it came to the kids, I had the mindset that as long as I did everything right, the kids would turn out. I poured myself into parenting books and manuals, practicing and perfecting my parenting techniques with fervor. I would fret and worry over every mistake I made, for surely my mistakes would be the ruin of our children.

One day, when I had whipped myself into a proper frenzy, I went to the Lord again, seeking wisdom. The Lord gave me a word of gracious and loving deliverance that day. He said, "Tamara, my children, Adam and Eve, had me as their example, and they failed. What makes you think your children aren't going to fail with you as their example?" I accepted God's message. His children failed even with complete access to His perfect example, and no matter what I do, my children will have failures too.

This realization redirected me from a place of fear and perfectionism in parenting (and relationships in general) to relying on the discernment and wisdom of God. Parenting with fear is hurtful and unloving—yes, *unloving!*

Second Timothy 1:7 actually contrasts love with fear and worry: "For God has not given us a spirit of fear, but of power and of love and of a sound mind" (NKJV).

Conducting any relationship with fear deprives us of power, love, good judgment, and self-control. When fear replaces these relationship essentials, a seed of bitterness is planted and spreads throughout the home. So how can we be brave in parenting, relationships, and life? We're often advised to "just give it to God." What does that mean?

Philippians 4:6–8 gives us a perfect prescription for release from fear and anxiety.

> Be anxious for nothing, but in everything by prayer and supplication, with thanksgiving, let your requests be made known to God; and the peace of God, which surpasses all understanding, will guard your hearts and minds through Christ Jesus. Finally, brethren, whatever things are true, whatever things are noble, whatever things are just, whatever things are pure, whatever things are lovely, whatever things are of good report, if there is any virtue and if there is anything praiseworthy-meditate on these things. (NKJV)

Praying your specific requests and concerns to God with thanksgiving brings unexplainable peace! Verse 8 goes further to tells us how to actually *replace* anxious thoughts. In the throes of fear, sit down with verse 8, and specifically think on something from each category listed. Write them down. Carry them around. Do it every day. Commit the verses to memory. Be intentional about abolishing fear. Be brave.

Bit of Brave Use this space to write Philippians 4:6–8.

*B*rave girl, you made it today, and today is what matters. Good job! Today, Dusty Duncan is at our table. Don't you love her name? There is nothing dusty about this brave girl. She is a wife and mom living in Garden City, Michigan.

Day Twenty-Seven

The LORD himself goes before you and will
be with you; he will never leave you nor forsake
you. Do not be afraid; do not be discouraged.

—Deuteronomy 31:8

In November 2013, my husband and I felt a call to adopt a child from China. Questions instantly swirled through our minds. *Can I love a child who was not born from my own womb? Would our two sons be able to accept an adopted child into our family? Can we afford to adopt internationally?* The list of questions went on from there. We lifted the thought of adoption up in prayer, and with a resounding "yes" from the Lord, we decided to go forward. Despite my questions, I strapped on my brave girl boots and took a step out in faith—but not without asking the Lord to go before us and remain in us.

One night, I sat at my kitchen table, and an e-mail came from our home study agency with an unexpected bill. At that moment, I crumbled into a heap of wild emotions and asked my husband how we were going to afford it all. He reassured me that God would get us through. So I sat down and just started to pray. "God, You have this, right? I don't, and I need your help." The next morning, I received a call at work from my husband saying we had received a donation that exceeded the bill I was crying over the night before. Praise the Lord!

In all of this, I have learned that I may not have all the answers. I may not know where the funds are going to come from next. I may not even know if, when I hold my baby girl in my arms on that one amazing day, she will bond with me or push me away. But I do know that my loving Father goes before me and clears the way.

To be brave is not always to be a fierce warrior, but to step out in faith, trusting that the Creator of the universe has already gone before me and cleared the way. I look forward to the unveiling of this calling for our lives. I will smile and praise the Lord when I look into her eyes and can say, "The Lord gave you to me."

Bit of Brave Are you or someone you know waiting on the journey of adoption? Take a moment to pray for that person this morning. The wait can grow weary. Be thankful that God never slumbers.

*ood morning, brave girl. Maybe if you're like me, the most you can squeak out is, "Mornin'." Either way, you are here, and I'm thrilled. The coffee is extra bold today, just like Beckie Nemcheck. Beckie is a wife, mom, and grandmother.

Day Twenty-Eight

When I am afraid, I will trust in You.

—Psalm 56:3

Trust = Bravery

I've lived through many trials in my life, struggles that I never expected to have to go through—things that no one should have to experience. Despite having survived this, I've never thought of myself as particularly brave. Am I a survivor? Definitely. Am I brave? Not so much. Over the course of my adult life, I've had most things pretty much planned out. I can now see how this sense of control brought a false sense of safety to my life. I've made sure not to rock the boat too much, to keep everything on an even keel. The status quo is my friend.

One of the things I've been called to is women's ministry. I have the amazing privilege and responsibility to help mentor and counsel ladies. As I hear their stories and the struggles they experience, I will often remind them that they need to trust God—trust His plan for their lives when every ounce of them doesn't want to trust.

One day, after meeting with a young woman, God spoke to me—inaudibly, but loud and clear. *Where do* you *have to trust me in your life? Are you living your life in any way that you must rely completely on my provision? Do you talk a good game about trusting me yet set your life up in such a way that you don't really need to?* Ouch.

I've been wrestling with this question for a while now. In what way *do* I honestly have to trust God? Where do I rely completely on Him? Recently, I've dealt with some health issues. I've done much soul-searching through this, and God is showing me how all of the perfect plans I have mapped out for my life (that help give me a sense of safety) mean absolutely nothing. I realize what little control I truly have over anything. My perfect little world can change quickly, and I can do nothing about it except hold tight to Jesus.

God is teaching me much about trust through this season. I need to trust that He will lead me to the right doctor. He will heal me—or He may not. I need to trust His good and perfect plan for my life. I have to surrender my sense of control daily, to choose to trust daily.

This surrender is definitely a choice—some days an easy choice, some days not so easy. I'm learning that choosing to trust equals bravery. That little girl who survived so much was indeed brave. She will continue to *choose* to be brave, even now—through His strength. "In his hand is the life of every living thing and the breath of all mankind" (Job 12:10).

Bit of Brave Is there a specific area of your life that needs a fresh dose of faith?

*B*rave girl, you've come to the right place this morning. Julie Reitz is joining us with her story. She is a prayer warrior if I've ever met one. Julie is a wife living in Belleville, Michigan.

Day Twenty-Nine

I had just graduated from law school and had a good job as a corporate lawyer when God began to put a vision in my life to change jobs. The job was going out on my own in a small firm at which I had no health insurance and no salary. If I found the clients, then I got paid. I was single and had no other source of income.

Moving out of comfort into a sincere place of faith was the hardest struggle and decision of my life. But at the same time, I desperately wanted more in life and more of God. I wasn't sure if it was God, or if I was just crazy. So, I prayed and asked God, "Are You sure You want me to step out in faith like this, moving to a job with no guaranteed income?"

God spoke to my heart and said, "I will let you decide. If you are happy and want status quo, then stay where you are. If you want change, then move."

I still hadn't decided completely what I would do when one day, I was singing along with a song on the radio, and I felt God tell me to stop and actually listen to the words. "So long, status quo; I think I'll just let go. You make me want to be brave." I knew at that moment that God was calling me to more. He wanted me to be brave and trust Him. He wanted to move me into a deeper level of faith.

So I did it; I quit my job and moved into that place of faith. It wasn't easy, but in that time, I grew closer to God through trust and prayer, and my relationship with Him deepened. He took complete care of me and eventually moved me to the dream job I have now.

The Bible is full of people whom God called to be strong, courageous, and trusting when the circumstances looked impossible. But He never let them down. If He is calling you to be brave, take the leap, and trust Him. He won't let you fall, and when He catches you, it will be the best, most incredible experience you can imagine.

"Be strong and courageous. Do not be afraid or terrified because of them, for the LORD *your God goes with you; he will never leave you nor forsake you*" (Deuteronomy 31:6).

Bit of Brave Where is Jesus leading you today—not tomorrow, but today?

*B*rave Girl, can you believe we are at day thirty already? Yes! Autumn Thornsberry is in the house today. She is a single young woman growing up in a world that is very different from the one I grew up in. When not in college, she resides in Garden City, Michigan.

Day Thirty

In the month of August, I decided at eighteen to move 450 miles north to attend Northern Michigan University. I didn't know a single person, professor, or even the names on the buildings there.

Months into college, I realized that I wasn't having the time of my life. College wasn't what I had designed in my head. It was disappointing. I wasn't making friends, which wasn't normal for me, and my mind was stuck replaying my past memories at home. I felt like I didn't belong there, and I felt left out from my friends back home.

In this season of solitude, I decided to surrender all the stresses of classes, my complex thoughts, and my hurting heart to the Lord. If I have everything but God, I have nothing. If I have nothing but the Lord, I have everything.

We live in a culture that wants everything to happen in an instant, otherwise labeled a fast-food culture. We get everything almost instantly through our iPhones and extremely fast Wi-Fi. When things become frustrating, we leave; we close the app. At school, as I watched dozens of students drop out of classes (probably feeling the same feelings I did), I realized how important it was for me to endure.

It's very easy for us to say we have faith when things go smoothly. But in the moments of our lives that really require faith, we have a tendency to back down. I was completely out of my comfort zone, and I wasn't forming another one any time soon.

As I go through this time of reflection, often feeling very alone, I see God working at the most pure and raw parts of myself. It's almost the end of my first year at college, and signs are plastered across the hallways to begin registering for next year. I've been in this season eight months.

Last night, I read Exodus 14:14: "The Lord will fight for you; you need only to be still." I've read about many people who heard God's still, small voice, and I always sought a moment like that. Today in class, I heard God say, "Stay. Be still. Stop moving." Bravery for me is simply staying right here, completely out of my comfort zone. I'm detached from my friends and family, just seeking out what the Lord has right here.

Bit of Brave Sometimes in our own fear, we can hold people back. Who do you need to let go of so they can find their own way to courage?

*G*ood morning, sunshine! It's a great day to be a brave girl! Margie Maierle is in the kitchen, cooking up a full breakfast. One of her love languages is feeding people. Aren't we fortunate? Margie is a mom living in Lincoln Park, Michigan.

Day Thirty-One

The mountains of Haiti are beautiful, and many look to climb them. I am a city girl, have weak ankles, and did I mention I am out of shape? Pom Mountain looked like something that I could never climb. But my team all wanted to go. Even though I was scared of falling behind, keeping everyone else behind, and falling or twisting my ankle, I went anyway.

It was steep, and I was really scared (and we only went about twenty feet). So I admit it—I let the fear of falling overtake me and told everyone to go ahead. I turned back and slid down the mountain (yes, I fell) but tried not to make a big deal of it. It had already been an emotional day, and I was thankful for sunglasses so no one could see I was crying.

I went back to the church where all the kids were, sat down with them, and listened to them sing and laugh. I taught them how to high-five and bump-explode their knuckles. We laughed and tried to communicate even though we couldn't understand each other, so we settled for holding hands and snuggling in the ninety-degree heat.

I was brave enough to try and brave enough to know that I needed to turn back. At first, I looked at it as a failure because everyone else went, and I turned back. But honestly, I was exactly where God called me to be— with the children on the mountain, loving them just as He would. The memories of the children laughing and smiling and faces that said, *I don't know what you are saying* are among the greatest from my trip to Haiti.

I'll never be sorry for turning back. I know that one day, I will climb that mountain. But until then, I'll be thankful to believe God enough to know my place, whether it's on the side of a mountain, making food at a soup kitchen in Detroit, or loving hundreds of teenagers every week. He has me just where He wants me for such a time as this. "Dear children, let us not love with words or speech but with actions and in truth" (1 John 3:18).

Bit of Brave Has God turned an experience with defeat into a win for you? Share it here.

*G*ood morning, brave girl. You are walking a bit taller these days. Courage looks good on you. The coffee is ready, and we are ready for you. Traci Whiting-Isley is already at the table with a full mug, waiting to share. Traci is a wife and mom living in Willis, Michigan.

Day Thirty-Two

> I tell you my friends, do not be afraid of those
> who kill the body, but after that can do no
> more. But I will show you whom you should
> fear: Fear Him who, after killing the body, has
> the power to throw you into hell. Yes, I tell you,
> fear Him. Are not five sparrows sold for two
> pennies? Yet not one of them is forgotten by
> God. Indeed, the very hairs of your head are all
> numbered. Don't be afraid; you are worth more
> than many sparrows.
>
> —Luke 12:4–7

In researching for this project, I discovered something. If you search for the word "fear" in the Bible, there are 336 references, 205 for the word "afraid," ninety-one for "terror," and forty-eight for "terrified." When you search for the word "courage," there are only thirty-three references and nineteen for "brave."

Obviously, we as people deal with feeling fear much more than we deal with feeling brave. I have wrestled with fear my whole life. I have felt inadequate because of it, paralyzed with it, and ashamed as a result of it. I also believed I was the only one who had a problem with it. Apparently, by looking at the sheer numbers, I was wrong.

What have I been afraid of? Honestly, I've feared you. I don't mean you personally; I mean people in general. I fear humans. Do I fear being physically attacked or killed? Am I afraid to leave the house or to let my children leave it? No, not really. I fear your opinion. I fear you will reject, ridicule, or dislike me.

In writing it out, I am struck with the realization that this is ludicrous. Yet the fear is real. It keeps me from speaking the words I need to say, sharing my God-given vision, and moving forward. Fear is very real. We all fear something. There would not be nearly seven hundred references to it in the Bible if this weren't true.

In my search, I only found fifty-two references to the words "courage" and "brave." There aren't many in comparison to "fear" and "terror." However, I discovered that there are seventy-one references to the word "comfort," 177 for "strength," 249 for "peace," and 533 for "love." That's nearly 1,100 verses that speak of the things that actually combat fear!

God understands us. He knows we fear. He has not left us with a bunch of commands not to fear and given us no reprieve or resource to draw from. No, He has given us everything we need and promised us comfort, strength, peace, and love over and over again. He knows we will fear and what we will need in those moments of fear. He may not take away our fears, but He has given us all we need to move forward in them.

There is a saying: "Do it afraid." I have prayed to be fearless and brave. But perhaps I'm praying for the wrong things. God does not expect me to be fearless; He expects me to move forward in spite of my fear. He has given me all I need to "do it afraid." So I will no longer pray to be fearless, but to be able to draw on Him and the resources He has provided for me. I will act, speak, share, and do what He has called me to do in spite of my fear.

Courage and bravery do not exist apart from fear. They come when we fear, but we move anyway. I hope you'll join me and "do it afraid." "Rise up; this matter is in your hands. We will support you, so take courage and do it" (Ezra 10:4).

Bit of Brave Are you ready to "do it afraid"?

Are you praying the following daily?

1. Pray daily for God to plant a seed of vision for your life.

2. Pray daily for the Holy Spirit to make you sensitive to see a need you can fill today.

3. Pray daily for the bravery to act upon that need.

*B*rave girl, we only have one week left together. I'm already sad when I think about it. Let's keep our focus on Jesus and finish this week strong. Liz Clark is joining us this morning to share her story of bravery. Liz is a wife and mom living in Belleville, Michigan.

Day Thirty-Three

What do you do when you are not a writer, not one to talk about the past? You know you have a story to tell; God keeps laying it on your heart. That quiet voice is not always quiet. "Someone out there needs to hear your story. What if you could help one person by sharing, give them hope for a future, let them know their life doesn't need to stay that way. It is possible to live a joy-filled life. They can have a life filled with happiness instead of tears. What if your story could do that for one person?"

It's time to put on my brave girl boots.

When we are young and naïve, we believe we know what is best. We think we are indestructible. This can lead to making wrong decisions, falling into the wrong crowd, or finding yourself in a dark place that you don't know if you can get out of. You judge yourself for the mistakes that you made. The feelings of worthlessness tell you that you do not deserve any better than the position you are in. When you are in that place, it's hard to find your way and know that you are worthy. At some point, you need to say, "Enough is enough," put those boots on, and tell yourself that you are worth more, because you are.

I found my way out of the darkness, but it took me longer to realize just how God was with me in every detail, keeping me safe. Things could have been so much worse for me. He was watching out for me. Through my mess, He showed unconditional love. For every day that I thought I was alone, He showed me that He was with me.

God wants more for us than we can ever dream! We need to be brave enough to look past our current circumstances to a future of freedom. Jesus will bridge that gap. Remember that He makes all things beautiful, including you and me. He has made us strong and worthy of love. A big, brave truth for me to realize is that I am *not* my past; it does *not* define me. You are not your past, no matter how often the enemy throws it in your face. You can change your future with God on your side, and it starts when you give Him control. From the moment you give it all to God, He will work things in your life that you never dreamed possible.

Fast-forward through time. I now have a loving husband of eighteen years who spoils me, three amazing children, and a wonderful church family! God has restored every day that the enemy took from me. He will do that for you. "This is my command—be strong and courageous! Do not be afraid or discouraged. For the LORD your God is with you wherever you go" (Joshua 1:9 NLT).

Bit of Brave Do you feel trapped in a situation with no solution in sight? Write a prayer to God about your need. He is listening.

*B*rave girl, we are celebrating thirty-four days today. Wow. I'm very thankful for you and glad we don't have to be brave alone. Cheryl Jones is consuming large amounts of iced coffee in the kitchen. Let's join her. Cheryl is a wife and mom living in Southgate, Michigan.

Day Thirty-Four

In 2008, at fifty years old, I rededicated my life to the Lord on my mom's deathbed. Within the next four months, Satan had a field day with my life. My mom died; I lost my career, and with that, a $67,000 salary. My husband and I lost our home and had to move into a two-bedroom apartment. My sister moved away, and I had to get rid of my dog.

Through all that, I felt amazing peace and love from my Heavenly Father. I held on to Jesus like crazy. In the months and years since then, I have forgiven my family, friends, husband, and myself.

In 2010, my husband and I moved to a new church. The Lord put us right where He needed us to be at the time. Jesus got a hold of me, and I have never looked back. I continue to pray for Him to lead me where He wants me to be. I've shared all of this to say one thing: God is faithful, even when we are not. He knows what our lives are all about today, tomorrow, and always.

I know in the storms of life, it sometimes feels like Jesus is not with us. His Word promises us that He is. He's refining us through the fires—and yes, that takes brave girl boots. Keep your eyes on the prize: the kingdom of God, where we can shed our boots, run to Him, and live forever in His glory land! "Have I not commanded you? Be strong and courageous. Do not be afraid; do not be discouraged, for the LORD your God will be with you wherever you go" (Joshua 1:9).

Bit of Brave Have you ever felt abandoned by God? Is there someone in your life who thinks that? Reach out to that person today. Remind this individual that God hasn't forgotten about her or him with a call, text, e-mail, or hug.

ive more days, brave girl! Laura Urenda joins us at our table this morning. If you brought ears to hear this morning, you'll be blessed. Laura is a wife living in Westland, Michigan.

Day Thirty-Five

This ol' gal has had to put on her brave girl boots quite a few times. Fear can be absolutely debilitating! I grew up in a place where fear-based decisions were common. A variety of abuses created an unyielding atmosphere of fear. This level of fear shaped me for a very long time and would remain a stronghold that would steal from me in both subtle and profound ways. But with God's help, sometimes with baby steps and at times with a few giant leaps, I've learned to face my fears. I've had to put on my brave girl boots when facing or kicking addictions, dealing with crippling anxiety, setting boundaries with people, sharing my faith, repenting to people I've hurt, stepping into unknown territories, and trusting God.

These are only a few from a list a mile long that I'm sure I could offer. The one thing they all have in common is that risk is involved. Being raised with trauma and abuse taught me to expect the rug to be ripped out from under me and for the next shoe to drop. What a horrible way to live!

This mindset affected everything, including my relationships, my ability to trust, and my ability to live peacefully and freely. But the fact is that regardless of where we come from, life has a way of throwing challenges at us. Challenges in general have a way of bringing out the best and often times the worst in us. Thankfully, when we allow God into our process, He uses everything for our good. "And we know that in all things God works for the good of those who love him, who have been called according to his purpose" (Romans 8:28).

God also promises to make our paths straight. "Trust in the Lord with all your heart and lean not on your own understanding; in all your ways submit to him, and he will make your paths straight" (Proverbs 3:5–6).

It is good to put on your brave girl boots! It's empowering! Once you've worn them, you will always know you can put them back on whenever needed. When we step into our fears, freedom awaits us. God is right there, saying, "You can do it!" So to fear, I say, "These boots are made for walking."

Bit of Brave How have you let fear define you?

*G*ood morning, brave girl! (Trust me; I'm not this perky in real life—at least not until after 10:00 a.m., and then I really start rockin'!) Michelle Tetreau is in the kitchen, cooking up a storm. She loves to cook, and it shows. You know where the cups are. Pour yourself one, and fix yourself a heapin' plate. You are with friends. Michelle is a wife, mom and grandma living in Taylor, Michigan.

Day Thirty-Six

Four and a half years ago, I lost my mother to nonalcoholic liver disease. I quickly became a major caregiver along with my dad, who was also not in good health. I had no choice but to pull up my brave girl bootstraps. I was also in constant conversation with God to get through the coming chain of events.

My parents were the greatest people you would ever want to meet. They instilled rich traditions; good, clean living; and belief in God that I rely on to this day. Ten months after losing my mom, my dad lost his battle with metastatic prostate cancer. It has been very hard to move on without them. It has, however, brought me even closer to God.

God has blessed me with the gifts of hospitality and compassion. Through all the love and support from friends, family, and the hospice teams we encountered on our journey with my parents, God has laid it on my heart to pursue a career in hospice care. I will graduate next May. Talk about being brave—returning to college after being out of school for twenty-some years took all the bravery I could muster up! God has really made me a brave girl! I am blessed beyond measure!

"Trust in the Lord with all your heart, and lean not on your own understanding; in all your ways submit to him, and he will make your paths straight" (Proverbs 3:5–6).

Bit of Brave Have you experienced a sad, hard time only to watch God make something beautiful from it? Share it here:

*G*ood morning, brave girl! Are you familiar with the movie *Brave*, with the redhead? Well, my friend Lisa Hildebrandt is over this morning, and she has curly red hair just like Merida. Lisa is a single woman living in Belleville, Michigan.

Day Thirty-Seven

I'm learning bravery in asking tough questions, in searching for God even during the horrible, awful, heartbreaking happenings in life. I'm learning to seek God's face in spite of my circumstances, no matter how painful they may be. Even if I don't like the answer or don't get an answer, I need to seek God's face. Even if the answer leads to more unanswered questions or it feels more like a betrayal than anything else, I need to seek God's face.

We've all been let down by people we love or disappointed with the God we love. What do we do? How do we get through? Do we just let it overwhelm us? I know that when things get too painful, I'm tempted to—and often do—shut down. If I don't want to face something, I find my escape in a million ways: books, movies, friends or isolation, shopping, eating greasy cheeseburgers, and watching marathons of old shows on Netflix—the list goes on and on. None of those things are what I really want, only distractions for that moment.

What if I pursued God through my pain instead, even if He's the one I feel betrayed or hurt by? I want to seek Him and trust His character even when what's happening makes no sense at all. I know and believe that what grieves me also grieves Him.

Lazarus died, and our Jesus wept. Be brave enough to, in the words of Sarah Bessey, "Stay there in the questions, in the doubts, in the wonderings and loneliness … your wounds and hurts and aches until, you are satisfied that Abba is there, too." Remember that the way the world is today is not how God intended it to be; it is a broken version. Remember that we have hope.

The word "remember" is often used in the Bible in reference to something God has promised will happen or something He has already done. I like to think of it as God saying, "I know you're freaking out. I know you don't understand, but remember Egypt? Remember the Red Sea? Remember the battles we've been through? Remember, you can trust Me. Remember, I am with you always. Remember, I will dry your tears."

This is where I'm learning to wear my brave girl boots. I'm learning to ask and seek, sit in the silence, and not know the whys but still run after my Jesus. I'm learning to trust Him through heartbreak and remember His faithfulness to me in the past. I'm also learning to believe, whether with eyes filled with tears or a heart full of joy, that He is faithful to me still. "I will remember the deeds of The Lord; yes, I will remember your miracles of long ago. I will consider all your works and meditate on all your mighty deeds" (Psalm 77:11–12).

Bit of Brave Have you been tempted to shut down when fear overwhelms you? In what ways do you shut down? What are some ways to push through those times?

ood morning, brave girl! We have two mornings left! We can do this. Your boots almost fit naturally. Kelly Bates is joining us for coffee this morning. She loves to recycle, so don't freak out if you see her going through my garbage. Kelly is a wife living in Westland, Michigan.

Day Thirty-Eight

Therefore everyone who confesses Me before
men, I will also confess him before My Father
who is in heaven. But whoever denies Me before
men, I will also deny him before My Father who
is in heaven.

—Matthew 10:32–33 (NASB)

I am a writer by no means. I have big thoughts in my head but struggle with the proper words to articulate what I would like to convey. That's where God came in this time. I thought, *Oh my goodness. Why did I reply yes when asked if I would write a devotional? What was I thinking?* I am not a Bible scholar, nor have I ever read the Bible from start to finish. Fortunately, I have great friends, family, pastors, mentors, small groups, teachers, and Bible study leaders to help me develop my relationship with God.

I felt a nudge from God directing me to share about women leading a dual life and being ashamed to walk with Him. So with bravery, here we go!

How often are you placed in a situation where you are at work, a friend's house, or even out in public when someone asks you to view an inappropriate video, tells you a dirty joke, or shares some gossip with you? What do you do in these situations? Do you watch the video and then share it with other people? Do you laugh at the dirty joke? Do you repeat the gossip?

As these circumstances present themselves, it takes bravery to stand firm in your beliefs and politely decline the advancement of any of these events.

Bravery says, "I am not worried about what people think of me. They will not be standing next to me on Judgment Day!" It can be very easy to get caught up in these types of scenarios. If I told you that I never have, I would be a liar. I think that's a whole other topic.

It can take time to develop this type of honest-to-your-faith-relationship, and none of us is perfect. We all fall short sometimes; that is our sin nature. Stand firm in your tests of faith, and be the light to others. Your coworkers, friends, and family may not have been shown the love of Jesus, so they may not even know the actions that they are committing are wrong.

Remember that the wicked one is a light sleeper and is always testing us. I encourage you to put on your brave girl boots in the face of the enemy. Like anything, it can become a habit if we practice it daily.

Bit of Brave Have you stood on your ground of faith boldly, or have you failed? What step can you take today to change areas that need improvement?

*G*ood morning, brave girl! Come on, and grab a mug. I don't want you to miss any of JaNiece Cook. JaNiece's personality shows up at the table before she does. JaNiece is a wife and mom living in Randallstown, Maryland.

Day Thirty-Nine

My parents taught me two very important life lessons. First, as an African-American woman, I need to work twice as hard to get what I want. No one will hand me anything. Second, God will always provide. These lessons have undoubtedly shaped the way I approach life as an adult. Being brave for me has never been an option. When it comes time to make tough decisions and step out completely in faith, God has instilled in me a strong, brave core.

So why invest in these brave girl boots now? It may seem like I've already got it figured out. Oh, not so, sista! This much-needed shoe-swapping has been eye-opening (or should I say, heart-opening). My brave girl journey is about God showing me that my bravery isn't just about *action*—it's about *surrender!* I've struggled all my life to be vulnerable. I'm not fake or phony, but I'm just guarded. It sounds kind of strange because I'm so outgoing, and I love to talk! The reality is that I've made a nice, comfortable spot here, behind my landscaped hedges.

There's no harm in being guarded. The problem is that I've made the mistake of bringing that practice into my relationship with God. I run to Him with open arms, saying, "Yes, I'll do!" and "Yes, I'll go!" I confidently take the big steps and put all my trust in Him. But He wants my heart—withholding nothing! He wants the deep, dark, quiet place that even I've avoided. With Him, it's not *do more, serve more, give more*. It's simple: just *be* more. Be more open. Be more vulnerable. Be totally surrendered.

I'm sure that I could step out of the boat in the midst of the storm like Peter (Matthew 14:22–23). That's the bravery I like! God does not seek external bravery without internal surrender. When I open my *whole* heart, He can take my big, bold, brave actions to show Himself in a new way and use me completely. "Surrender yourself to the Lord and wait patiently for Him" (Psalm 37:7a GW).

Bit of Brave Have you let God draw near to the secret places in your heart?

*O*h, sweet, brave girl! I can't help but feel a bit sad today. Come on in; it's just us at our table this morning. In a thousand ways, I'd love to tell you how proud I am of you. We made it to forty! How about we grab a cup of hot coffee one last time?

Day Forty

"Tami, go sit at the dummy table."

I had just finished sharing my book report on the Boston Tea Party when those words from my third-grade teacher's mouth pierced my heart and left a wound. Apparently, I hadn't done the book report correctly. Standing in front of my class, red-faced, trying to not let the tears welling up in my eyes fall in front of my classmates, I slowly made my way to the table.

Words are powerful. They can be life-giving and provide great encouragement to help us take on another day. They can also wound us with holes so deep in our souls that we begin to take matters into our own hands to ensure we never get wounded again. It shows up as self-preservation, self-reliance, and self-sufficiency. I wore those like a badge of honor. But those things were miserable attempts at a Band-Aid.

My eight-year-old self determined right then and there that I would believe the lie of the enemy and never put myself in a position to be made a fool of again. Throughout most of my life, I avoided any and all public speaking and anything I knew I wouldn't be good at. It was my way of controlling my life, playing things safe, protecting that wound at all costs.

These truth-filled lyrics from Francesca Battistelli's song "Free to Be Me" filled my ears this morning: "A war's already waged for my destiny, but You've already won the battle, and You've got great plans for me, though I can't always see." The war for my destiny was on.

Growing up, I never knew a holy God who battled for my life and had a plan for it. It's a plan that requires bravery on my part. I must stop holding the Band-Aid so He can pull it off and begin to heal me. Have you noticed that the "follow Me" adventure Jesus calls us to doesn't have room for self-preservation, self-reliance, or self-sufficiency? We need to pack light; all we need is found in Him.

I didn't know that what I avoided my whole life would be something God would call me to do for Him. No wonder my enemy tried his best to stop those plans. He may have stalled them, but he didn't have the power to stop them. Praise God!

Healing of any kind takes time. Over the years, God has poured heaps of anointed grace onto my wound. God has met me with His healing touch in His Word and also used godly influences like my pastor and his wife to help bring forth healing in my life.

What wounds do you carry today? Is your makeshift Band-Aid working for you? Trust me; I get it. I've lived it. It'll hurt when it's pulled off, but be brave enough to let God take if off and begin healing your wounds today. He is the only one who can. "He heals the brokenhearted and binds up their wounds" (Psalm 147:3).

Bit of Brave: Do you have a Band-Aid that needs removal? Are you willing to let God close enough to remove it? Tell Him here:

Brave girl, you are getting a bit used it now, aren't you? We've traveled some road together over the last forty days. To be honest, I'm going to miss you.

I wonder if you saw a piece of yourself in some, if not all, of these other brave girls. They are just like us: filled with fears and insecurity, each with a story to tell. These stories are of a loving, long-suffering God who met them in their need.

Fear is nothing new to God. His children have dealt with this thing for a long time. Skip through Scripture, and you will find plenty of instances where God encourages us to be brave and courageous. He knows our bent toward fear and not faith.

Is there a secret to bravery? When we look to Scripture, we'll see time and time again that the key is trusting God. Isaiah 26:4 says, "Trust in the LORD FOREVER, FOR THE LORD, THE LORD HIMSELF, IS THE ROCK ETERNAL."

Do you want a protector who never fails? Yes, please! Who wouldn't want that? Brave girl, seeking God with an undivided heart will change your life and provide a breeding ground for faith. This faith will appear not just at church or Bible study faith, but twenty-four/seven. There is no room for fear when you are full of faith. "Teach me your way, Lord, that I may rely on your faithfulness; give me an undivided heart, that I may fear your name" (Psalm 86:11).

Do you have time for one last cup of coffee? I'll share with you one more story about God and my growing pains of bravery. It was the hardest time but a tremendous time of growth in my life. It's funny how God works. We often hope that growing doesn't involve any growing pains. Giving birth to new life involves labor. Just ask any momma. I remember this season fondly now because Jesus met me every step of the way. We walked it out together. He doesn't play favorites, brave girl. He will meet you and walk it out with you too!

I remember like it was yesterday. "Tami, if I asked you to be single for Me, would you?" I felt the nudge of the Lord once again. It's the one I keep ignoring. Could it be? Could God really be asking me that question? What ever happened to Him giving me the desires of my heart? Am I not owed that? At the time, I was thirty-seven years old, never married—and yes, I thought God owed me that. I squirm just typing those words now, but it's truly how I felt. How is that for honesty?

I wish I could tell you I handled that well. I sure didn't. I kicked, screamed, and ugly cried. For several weeks, I put a brave face on publicly but cried buckets privately.

Having walked with the Lord for about five years, I was embarrassed by how badly that bothered me. "I'll do anything for You, Lord! My life is Yours, Jesus!" These are all great spiritual words until He takes you up on them, and then you realize they were just words. If I was really as spiritually mature as I thought I was, instead of kicking my feet, I would have said, "Yes, God." Everything changes when God takes us out of the classroom and on a field trip.

Because I had tasted and seen for myself how good the Lord was, I knew turning back was not an option. I spoke to Dave Stephens, a pastor at my church, who said, "God is asking if you would, not calling you. If you don't trust God with this, Tami, you will never be prepared for the next thing He asks you to trust Him with." I listened. I felt defeated, but I listened. It was time to put on my brave girl boots.

I got up the next morning, reality hanging on me like a noose, and realized I had to completely depend on God to walk this out. I knelt at my bed and began to pray for God to help me accept what felt like a bitter drink of sacrifice.

As soon as I knelt down, I felt very ashamed. I couldn't remember the last time I had knelt before my Lord. Remembering this now still stings my eyes with tears. I was a headstrong, self-sufficient leader who had forgotten just how much she needed her Savior. Almost as instantly as I felt shame, a rush of peace swept over me, and I was ministered to by the Holy Spirit. I knew that God was in all of this, and I needed to walk it out, wherever it may lead.

I began to pour myself into ministry at my church. I was the volunteer leader of our singles group. You know that saying, "Serve others, and your trials get smaller"? It's very true. God met me in my loneliness as I served others. Over time, I began to embrace a life of singleness. God was faithful to encourage me when I needed encouragement. He gave me everything I needed to get through each day. Guess what? I began to build a life as a sold-out single for God.

Over the next year, the Lord began to show my pastor, Rocky Barra, a call on my life for full-time ministry. In 2005, I left an eighteen-year career to join the staff of Connection Church as Connection Director. The advice I had received a year prior rang the bell of truth in my heart. Leaving my career was very easy, because God had already built a foundation of trust with me. He is a very good Father.

Fast-forward six years: I felt the Lord prompt me (more like shake my shoulders) to take a study called *Changes That Heal* by Henry Cloud. Other than the Word of God, no other book has come close to changing my life. During the course of this study, I began to understand some of my behaviors and why I thought the way I did. It really changed my life. Doing the work of not only self-examination, but also putting into practice what I learned was a humbling and hard experience. When we acknowledge our need for God, He shows up in a big way. You can count on it, brave girl. God began changing me into an open, connected person.

Soon after completing that study, I felt an old, familiar stirring in my heart; I wanted to be married. I looked at marriage differently now. I no longer looked for someone to complete me and be a little god for me by filling in the gaps. I now fully understood that Jesus completes me. I wasn't looking for a soul mate; I was looking for someone to run my race of faith with. That's just not Christian chatter; I deeply believed that to be true. When we seek God wholeheartedly, things change. We go in hoping our situations change. But really, *we* do. God is so stinkin' smart. What I initially considered to be a season of loss, God used to prune and prepare my life for what He had for me. That pruning continues today.

Taking responsibility for your life is the big theme of *Changes That Heal*. The notion of getting out there and making myself available to meet Christian men was daunting, but I knew it was a necessary step. I put myself out there but didn't meet anyone. One day, I asked God how to pray about this. I felt I had done the hard work to get ready for something or someone, and nothing was happening.

Do you ever feel that way? It's a tough season to be in. Many days, I felt like I was on the runway, and the call to take off wasn't coming. I was directed to Lamentations 3:24: "I say to myself, 'The LORD is my portion; therefore I will wait for him.'" Each time I felt dissatisfaction rise up in me, I quickly spoke that Scripture aloud, and those thoughts were taken captive. I chased after God wholeheartedly. I didn't have to run very far; He was right there. God will do amazing things in and through a heart totally devoted to Him.

On a whim, I joined an online dating service. I was not sure what to expect but thought I would try it. In April 2011, I met a great man named Cal Walker. We began dating, and over a lot of long drives, large diet Cokes, and long talks, we fell in love. I know I'm a bit partial, but it doesn't get much better than Cal. He is romantic, writes me poetry, and brushes my hair. Love and laughter are his calling card. As wonderful as all those things are, the greatest thing about Cal is his commitment to the Lord. Cal deeply loves Jesus. Was Cal worth the wait? I would have gladly waited another twenty years to meet him.

In March 2012, walking around Milford, Michigan on a snowy evening, Cal took my hands in his, dropped to one knee, and said, "You've made me so happy. I will never leave you. I will never raise a hand against you, and I want to live with you the rest of my life. Will you marry me?"

On August 3, 2013, one week shy of my forty-sixth birthday, a never-married, single woman became Mrs. Cal Walker. Without a doubt, we believe our union was orchestrated by God. Faith in God means having faith in His timing. As hard as that is for us to embrace, God is an on-time God.

Had Cal and I met in 2004 when I so desperately wanted to be married, Cal wouldn't have been interested in me. I had a rough edge to me that he wouldn't have been drawn to. When the time was right, we were very compatible—both in our walks with God and how we live and love in everyday life.

My entire life changed when I began to seek God with an undivided heart. Fear began to dwindle, and faith took its place. Whatever road you walk today, if fear is your companion, I get you. If most people were transparent with you, they would say the same thing. You'll find no judgment here, just encouragement that there is a better way.

I've walked the lonely road of singleness. I know the tears some women cry when no one is around or the thought, *Is he the one?* that races through some women's minds each time they meet an eligible man. I've lived it; I get it.

Sometimes, I think we hold on to fear because there is a part of us that thinks, *What God wants to give me, I probably won't like anyway.* So we hold on to fear and forego faith. That is a lie. Fear is a liar.

I want to leave you with some encouragement and bacon, because everything goes better with bacon. During my long single season, I went through a fast-food drive-through to grab a quick bite to eat. In my head, I was almost yelling, "I want a burger with bacon and gooey sauce. That's what I want!" I hadn't had red meat like that in over a year, and that's what I wanted! However, when it was my turn to order, I did the *right* thing and ordered the healthiest choice, a grilled chicken wrap. I pulled into a parking spot, opened my bag, and couldn't believe what I saw—not one, but two Angus beef, cheese, bacon, gooey sauce wraps. Brave girl,

I never even said that aloud! It took my breath away and scared me for a second. Then I quickly came to my senses and ate both!

Psalm 84:11 (ESV) tells us, "For the Lord God is a sun and shield; the Lord bestows favor and honor. No good thing does he withhold from those who walk uprightly." Sweet friend, if God cares enough to give this girl some bacon, don't you think that the plans He has for you are good?

I had to learn the hard way that every prayer I pray will not be answered in my timing or in my way. I have learned that every prayer will be answered with my best in mind. God doesn't withhold blessing just to withhold blessing. A lot of my wants can be shortsighted. I have no idea what my future holds. God does, though.

During that long season of singleness, one of the greatest gifts God gave me was the prompting to take full advantage of my single years. In that season, I tackled my issues from childhood, reduced my financial debt substantially, and paid attention to my health. I also sought the Lord wholeheartedly and watched Him change me from the inside out.

Brave girl, He didn't waste a day.

God is trustworthy and faithful. Fear would have kept me immature and just plain stuck.

Walk this out, brave girl, one trembling step at a time, hand in hand with the God who never trembles. "Since God assured us, 'I'll never let you down, never walk off and leave you,' we can boldly quote, 'God is there, ready to help; I'm fearless no matter what. Who or what can get to me?'" (Hebrews 13:6 MSG)

Are You a child of God?

God has created every single one of us. You are God's beautiful creation. It would be easy to toss a generalized blanket across all of us and say, "We're all children of God," but the hard news to hear is that we aren't.

There is one thing separating you from a relationship with God, and that's sin. Romans 3:23 tells us, "For all have sinned and fall short of the glory of God." Not just a few people, but all people have sinned—but there is good news. The invitation into the family of God is an open one. There are no background checks, profiling, or exclusions. All are welcome—anyone and everyone!

This is possible through faith in Jesus Christ. In Romans 10:9 (NASB), we'll find this promise: "if you confess with your mouth Jesus as Lord, and believe in your heart that God raised Him from the dead, you will be saved."

John 1:12 says, "Yet to all who did receive him, to those who believed in his name, He gave the right to become children of God."

Are you a child of God? The Scriptures above give us the answer. Have you received Him? Do you believe in His name? "See what great love the Father has lavished on us, that we should be called children of God! And that is what we are! The reason the world does not know us is that it did not know him" (1 John 3:1).

The great love the Father has lavished on us is grace—unmerited favor. We can't work our way or earn access into the family of God.

Jesus makes it possible for us to be in a relationship with God, the Father. "Repent, then, and turn to God, so that your sins may be wiped out, that times of refreshing may come from the Lord" (Acts 3:19).

In 2 Corinthians 7:10 we're told, "Godly sorrow brings repentance that leads to salvation and leaves no regret, but worldly sorrow brings death."

When we acknowledge our need to have our sins wiped out by turning to the Lord, receiving Him, and believing in His name, we can be children of God. You can make that decision today. Ask Jesus to come into your life as Savior, Lord, and King, and begin walking with Him today.

If you've asked Jesus to be your Savior today, please let us know. We want to celebrate with you! Contact us at *hello@CGgirls.org.*

About CGgirls

Ideas usually start as answers to questions. In 2009, I asked, "What would happen if women left their generational and denominational differences at the door and just became girls who loved God?" We would find our common ground. On our common ground, we could harness this unity, take God's love from the pews to the pavement, and change our world.

It's that simple. Walking in step with God and in unity and love for one another can be a powerful force that leaves His fingerprints on changed lives outside of our church walls.

This is no longer just an idea; it's happening. Four times a year, women from over thirty metro Detroit area churches gather on their common ground for a girl's night with a God focus. At each of our events, you'll find a worship team comprised of different churches and a speaker with a story or message that will point you to Christ.

Each CG event has a different outreach spotlight, and hundreds of items are donated by CGgirls. We end the night with a fantastic afterparty where women get a chance to connect with other women.

You can keep up with CGgirls at *www.cggirls.org,*
www.twitter.com/comgro, and
www.facebook.com/commongroundgirls.

About Brave Girl Boots

A spark started as a sixty-day prayer challenge for the women of CGgirls. All those who participated received a morning devotional in their inboxes along with a challenge to pray daily. Women were encouraged to

1. Pray daily for God to plant a seed of vision for their lives.
2. Pray daily for the Holy Spirit to make them sensitive to see needs they could fill that day.
3. Pray daily for the bravery to act upon these needs.

That tiny spark grew into a full forest fire as women began to put their brave girl boots on and trust God in areas where they had never trusted Him before.

We heard stories from women who knew they needed to be better moms, and stories of relationship reconciliation started pouring in. We quickly saw that God was indeed up to something as women began to take the hand of faith and let go of the hand of fear.

Our hope of expanding this platform by writing *Brave Girl Boots* is to encourage you to share your own stories of brave and not-so-brave moments with others. We'd love to hear your stories too! Please share them with us at *www.bravegirlboots.org.*

Made in the USA
Middletown, DE
02 November 2017